BEAT
TEXAS
HOLD'EM

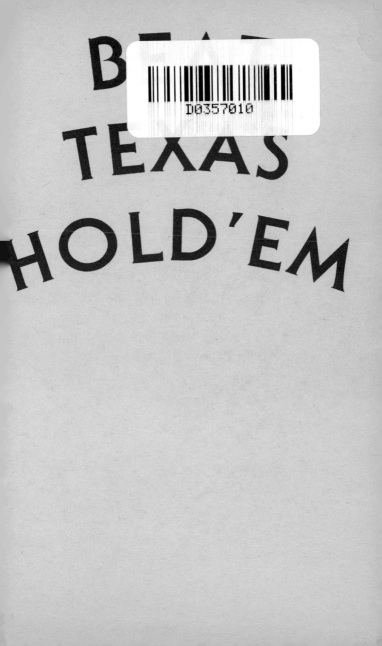

BEAT TEXAS HOLD'EM

INTERNET ◆ TOURNAMENT ◆ LIMIT & NO-LIMIT GAMES

TOM McEVOY
SHANE SMITH

CARDOZA PUBLISHING

Cardoza Publishing is the foremost gaming and gambling publisher in the world with a library of more than 100 up-to-date and easy-to-read books and strategies. These authoritative works are written by the top experts in their fields and with more than 7,500,000 books in print, represent the best-selling and most popular gaming books anywhere.

First Edition

Copyright ©2004 by Tom McEvoy and Shane Smith
- All Rights Reserved -

ISBN: 1-58042-150-4
Library of Congress Catalog No: 2004109833

Visit our web site (www.cardozapub.com) or write for a full list of Cardoza books and advanced strategies.

CARDOZA PUBLISHING
P.O. Box 1500, Cooper Station, New York, NY 10276
Phone (800)577-WINS
email: cardozapub@aol.com
www.cardozapub.com

ABOUT THE AUTHORS

Tom McEvoy, the 1983 World Champion of Poker, has won four World Series titles. He is the author of the acclaimed *Championship Tournament Poker*, "one of the most important poker books of all time," and co-author of 10 other titles including *No-Limit Texas Hold'em*, *Championship No-Limit & Pot-Limit Hold'em*, *Championship Stud*, *Championship Omaha*, *Championship Satellite Strategy*, *The Championship Table*, *Championship Tournament Practice Hands* and *Championship Hold'em*.

Shane Smith is one of the most highly regarded writers in the poker world and is a top low-limit tournament player. In addition to writing several best-selling books, including *Poker Tournament Tips from the Pros*, Smith served as editor of two gaming magazines and co-authored and ghosted more than 10 books with some of the top experts and writers in poker, including T.J. Cloutier, Cowboy Wolford, and World Poker Champions Tom McEvoy and Brad Daugherty.

TABLE OF
CONTENTS

"Luck is like lightning. You can't bottle it and you never know when or where it will strike. So that leaves skill, and if you want to become a winner at poker you'd better start developing some." -- **Bobby Baldwin**

"The main reason people fail to accomplish as much as they could—in poker and in life—is that they don't play their best game." -- **Mike Caro**

"Smile and take the money, remembering that it's better to win a small pot than to lose a big one." -- **Roy West**

"If the cards break even, a good player will win the money because he makes fewer mistakes than a bad player makes." -- **T.J. Cloutier**

"If you take poker seriously, then you ought to treat it like a business. But who says you have to take it seriously? Poker is great recreation." -- **Doyle Brunson**

Introduction

Introduction

A humble accountant from Tennessee, a polished Ph.D. from California, a colorful Vietnamese refugee—what do they all have in common? Each of these poker players beat Texas hold'em for $1 million or more at the World Series of Poker. Want to join them in the winner's circle? You've come to the right place. *Beat Texas Hold'em* shows you how to win your share of the gold and the glory by learning how to play poker's most glamorous game.

You've watched poker on television, and maybe you've played hold'em around your kitchen table with the neighbors or dabbled with it on the Internet. Now you want to give it a serious shot. World Champion of Poker Tom McEvoy and acclaimed poker author Shane Smith teach you how to join the ranks of the winners who play for megabucks in World Poker Tour and World Series of Poker televised hold'em games.

First you'll learn the basics of Texas hold'em so that you can practice playing the game at home before you venture into a casino or an online poker room. Next we give you our top 10 secrets for winning *limit* hold'em games, plus a bonus 10 practice hands that show you how to play particular card combinations you are dealt.

Limit hold'em is a lot safer game for beginners to start playing because you can bet only a fixed amount of money at one time.

Once you've mastered when to hold'em and when to fold'em in limit poker, you'll probably want to learn how to beat poker's glamour game, *no-limit* hold'em, in which the amount of money you can bet is limited only by the number of chips you have stacked up in front of you. Tom's top 10 tips and 10 practice hands guide you through the mine fields of this explosively exciting game.

Next comes instruction on how to play hold'em without leaving the comfort of your home—on the Internet in your pajamas! Tom guides you through the process of setting up an online account, logging onto a poker room in cyber space, and learning how to beat Texas hold'em even though you can't look your virtual opponents in the eyes.

Texas hold'em tournaments are television's most thrilling and lucrative games, and the authors want you to win your rightful share of the action. Their top 10 tips for winning hold'em tournaments teach you how to enjoy the thrill of victory and minimize the agony of defeat in poker's biggest money game by learning important tournament tactics that will beat even the craftiest opponents.

"How Would You Play This Hand?" is an added bonus to each section of *Beat Texas Hold'em*. Tom gives expert answers on how to play problem hands in real situations that have stumped actual players who have asked him for help throughout his illustrious poker career. Shane's review questions are designed to give you a fast-take on the important concepts of each form of Texas hold'em.

And if you want to "talk the talk," you'll find the glossary of poker terms designed especially for new hold'em players a great resource.

Enough of this rah-rah introduction—now let's beat Texas hold'em! All it takes is enough skill, a little bit of luck, and a lot of courage. Tom and Shane are waiting to shake hands with you in the winner's circle one day soon.

How Texas Hold'em is Played

Overview

If you've never played Texas hold'em, poker's most exciting game, buckle up! You're in for the ride of your life with the "Cadillac of poker," the nickname that Doyle Brunson, the world's most famous poker player and the author of *Super System*, gave it. No other form of poker has captured the imagination of the public like Texas hold'em—just ask the millions of viewers who watch The World Series of Poker and the World Poker Tour hold'em tournaments on television every week.

But as thrilling as it is to see other people push mountains of chips into the center of the table and win megabucks, it's even more exciting when you're in the middle of the action yourself, playing poker's hottest game.

Here's a brief overview of how the game is played. We'll paint a more vivid picture in the next part of this section.

Texas hold'em, which is also commonly referred to as simply **hold'em**, is a form of high poker in which the player with the highest five-card combination at the end of the deal wins the **pot**, the money that players have wagered and which sits in the middle of the table. The pot is what every player tries to win on each deal.

Each player is dealt two personal cards, called **hole** cards, face down, which he combines with five community cards, the

board, that are dealt face-up in the middle of the table to make his best possible five-card hand.

The best hand in Texas hold'em is a **royal flush**, A-K-Q-J-10 in the same suit. The second-best hand is a **straight flush**, any five cards of the same suit in sequence, followed by **four-of-a-kind**, four cards of the same rank such as 7-7-7-7.

Following these top three hands are a **full house**, three cards of the same rank plus two cards of a second rank, a **flush**, five cards in the same suit, a **straight**, five cards in sequence such as K-Q-J-10-9, **three-of-a-kind**, three cards of the same rank, **two pair**, two groups of cards of equal rank such as J-J and 9-9 (jacks over nines), and **one pair**, one group of equally ranked cards such as K-K.

If none of the other combinations are held, then the **high card** of the five best cards will win. For these purposes, the ace represents the highest card, the deuce the lowest. If both players have the same high cards, then the next lowest of high card will determine the winner and so on down till one card prevails over another. For example, K-Q-J-8-7 is higher ranked than K-Q-10-8-7, the jack counting as a higher card than the ten since the kings and queens are commonly held.

To start a round of betting, the dealer gives you and every other player in the game two hole cards face down. When it's your turn to **act**, you can do one of three things—fold, call or raise.

If you don't like your hole cards, you can **fold** by gently sliding them back to the dealer. Folding indicates that you do not wish to match the bets required and opt out of play.

Or you can **call** by matching the size of the required bet, or **raise** by increasing the size of the bet. These latter two actions, calling and raising, keep you active in the hand.

If all players fold when a player bets or raises, the remaining player, by default, wins the pot. This can happen at any point during a hold'em hand.

After every player has acted, if at least two players are remaining to contest the pot, the dealer places three community cards face up in the center of the table. This is called the **flop**. Every player who didn't fold before the flop is active and can participate in the betting. The first player to act may either check—not wager and pass play on to the next player while still remaining active—or initiate play by betting, placing a wager into the pot.

Once any player has bet, then the other active players must either fold, call or raise. If all players check, then the betting is closed for the round.

Then the dealer puts a fourth community card, called the **turn**, in the middle of the table, followed by another round of betting with players having the usual options—checking, betting, raising or folding.

Finally, the dealer turns up the fifth and final community card, called the **river**, followed by one last round of betting.

Then there is the **showdown**, where the remaining players show their cards and the best hand wins all the money in the pot, or if the pot is tied, then the money is divided evenly.

When a hand is concluded and the winner has claimed the pot—either through other players folding and leaving a default winner, or by having the best hand at the showdown—the dealer reshuffles the cards and deals a new hand.

Texas hold'em is played in two different formats called **cash** or **side** games and **tournament** games. If you are playing in a cash game and lose all your money, you can reach into your pocket for more money and buy additional chips to stay in action. But if you lose all your chips in a tournament, you cannot buy in for any more, that's it, you're done for the day.

Hold'em also is played with two different betting structures. If you are playing **limit hold'em**, the amount of money you can bet at any one time is limited to a prescribed amount.

There are all sorts of betting structures, depending upon the amount of money people wish to wager, usually in a two-tier amount such as $5-$10, where the lower tier, the $5 in this example, is the required amount for bets and raises (no more, no less) before the flop and on the flop; and the higher tier, the $10 (again, no more and no less), is the required size of bets and raise on the turn and river.

But if you are playing **no-limit hold'em**, your bet is limited only by the amount of money you have in front of you—and you can bet it all at one time if you want to.

Sounds simple, doesn't it? Yes, it is. Texas hold'em takes only a few hours to learn—but as the old pros say, it takes a lifetime to master the game.

Forget that "lifetime" bit, we're here to help you shorten your learning curve by several decades. Even novice players with minimum knowledge and some poker sense are winning money in online and casino Texas hold'em games. And a player who had never before played no-limit hold'em in a casino won the World Series of Poker in 2003 to the tune of $2.5 million. With that music ringing in your ears, let's learn how to play the game. After all, you can't win it if you're not in it!

Basics of Play

The Deal

Each player is dealt two cards face down, beginning with the player sitting to the left of the **button**. The button is a small disc that indicates who the "dealer" is. It is used by the casino dealer so that he can keep track of who the dealer would be if players dealt the cards themselves, like they used to do in the old days of casino poker and the way people still do in home games.

At the start of every new deal, the casino dealer moves the button one seat to the left. When the button has traveled all the way around the table, one **round** of play has been completed.

Posting the Blinds

The first person to the left of the button is called the **small blind** and must post a predetermined bet in front of him before the deal. The second person to the left of the button is called the **big blind**. The big blind must post a prescribed bet before the deal that is double the amount of the small blind.

The purpose of posting blind bets is to stimulate action. That is, the blinds get the pot started so that there will be some money to compete for. Sometimes the blinds force people to play hands they would not have played if they hadn't already been required to put money into the pot.

In cash games, the amount of money that you must post when it's your turn to be the big blind or the small blind remains the same throughout the game. In tournaments, the size of the blinds increases at the beginning of each new **level** (a set length of time during which the blinds remain the same).

In some tournaments, a level remains at the same size of blinds for only 20 minutes. In others, the levels may stay the same for one hour or more. But one thing's for sure: If you never play a hand, you will eventually go broke just from paying the two blind bets that you are forced to post during each round of play.

The Types of Hands to Play

In both limit hold'em and no-limit hold'em, big pairs and high cards rule the roost. Two aces, two kings, two queens, two jacks, and A-K are **premium hands**.

You would like to have a pair in your hand and then see one of your rank come on the flop. You also can play other types of hands in different circumstances, but these premium hands are the best ones to play. In limit hold'em, you can play more types of hands than you can in no-limit hold'em. For example, suited connecting cards such as Q♥ J♥ or 10♦ 9♦ are more valuable hands in limit hold'em games than they are in no-limit hold'em games.

Betting

The Four Betting Rounds

Betting begins after you have been dealt your two **hole** cards (your hand) face down. The first player who must act is the person who is sitting immediately to the left of the Big Blind. The action continues clockwise with everyone acting in turn. The Big Blind is the last player to act. When he has finished acting, the first round of betting is over. After the round of betting is over, the dealer puts three community cards, the

flop, face-up in the center of the table and the second round of betting begins.

This time, the first active player to the left of the button must act first. Then each player who did not fold before the flop can check, bet, call a bet, raise, reraise or fold when it is his turn to act.

After the betting on the flop is finished, the dealer places a fourth community card, called **fourth street** or the **turn**, face-up in the center of the table, followed by another round of betting. Then he deals the final community card, called **fifth street** or the **river**, face-up in the center and there is a final round of betting.

The Size of the Bets

The size of the bet or raise that you can make when it's your turn to act depends on whether you are playing **limit** Texas hold'em or **no-limit** Texas hold'em.

In **limit hold'em**, the number of chips that you can bet is limited to a fixed upper limit. The upper limit on the first two rounds of betting is the size of the big blind.

For example, if the big blind is $4, the most you can bet or raise before the flop and on the flop is $4. On the third and fourth rounds of betting, the limit usually doubles to twice the size of the big blind. For example, if the big blind is $4, you must bet $8 on the turn and river. This game would be called "4-8" hold'em.

Similarly, you might find 5-10, 10-20, 15-30, 100-200 and many other betting levels. Casinos and card rooms typically offer many levels for players to choose from.

In **no-limit hold'em**, you can bet your entire stack of chips on any of these betting rounds. If you decide to bet all your chips at once, you announce, "I'm going all in!" and push all your chips into the center of the table. An opponent can call your all-in bet even if he doesn't have as many chips as you have bet. In that case, the size of the bet can be no bigger than the smaller stack. If you have the bigger stack and lose the hand, you get to keep the remaining chips in your stack.

For example, suppose you have $6,000 in chips and go all in against Player B, who has $4,000 in chips. Alas, Player B wins the pot at the showdown. But here's the good news: He is eligible to win only an amount that is equal to his original wager. Therefore you get a refund of $2,000 in chips because Player B could only call $4,000 of your original wager.

The Betting Sequence for Limit Texas Hold'em

In a typical $4-$8 limit hold'em game, the blinds are $2-$4 (one-half the amount of the minimum-maximum bets). The maximum amount that you can bet or raise on the first two betting rounds is $4. On the deal (before the flop), the first player to act can fold, call by placing $4 in chips in the center of the table, or raise by placing $8 in chips in the middle. If someone raises before it is your turn to act, you can fold, call the raise by putting in $8, or reraise to $12. On the flop (the second betting round), the bets are again limited to $4 increments.

The size of the bet doubles on the turn card (the fourth community card) and the river card (the fifth community card). For example, if you are the first player to act on the turn, you must bet $8, no more and no less. If someone bets before it's your turn to act, you can raise to $16, no more and no less. Card rooms usually allow three or four raises on each round of betting.

Because limit hold'em has fixed betting limits, most low-limit hold'em players feel comfortable playing this ever-popular form of hold'em. They know the minimum amount of money it will cost them to play a hand if the pot isn't raised, and can judge whether they want to pay the maximum it will cost to play if the pot is raised.

Casinos spread far more limit Texas hold'em games than no-limit games because they know that players' bankrolls last longer when the betting limits are fixed. No-limit hold'em is a horse of a different color, a game in which you can lose your entire stake on one hand.

The Betting Sequence for No-Limit Texas Hold'em

No-limit hold'em is the poker game that you most often see being played on television tournaments. In contrast to limit hold'em where you can bet only a fixed amount, you can bet as much money as you want to gamble with in no-limit hold'em.

Suppose the size of the small blind is $1,000 and the big blind is $2,000 at the championship table of a World Poker Tour tournament you're watching on television. The dealer has just dealt two cards to each player. He has not dealt any community cards yet. The player sitting to the immediate left of the big blind is the first person to act. He has to match the size of the big blind (**call**) if he wants to play his cards. In this example, $2,000 is the least that he can bet in order to play the hand.

If he wants to raise, he must bet at least double the amount of the big blind ($4,000 in this example). The player can also raise any amount up to the number of chips he has in his stack. For example, if he has $80,000 in front of him, he can raise to $30,000 by announcing, "Raise to $30,000." Or he can bet his entire $80,000 by announcing, "All in."

A player who does not have enough chips to call the minimum bet can still play the hand by putting in all the chips he has left in his stack. For instance, if he only has $3,000 in chips, he can call with everything he has by announcing that he is all in. At the end of the fourth betting round (the river), the player with the best hand wins all the chips in the middle of the table (the pot).

Here's the risky part of playing no-limit hold'em—you can lose all your money on a single bet. It takes a different breed of cat to be willing to take that big a risk, but it sure makes the game exciting to watch on television!

Of course, no-limit hold'em is played in tournament mode only on TV, which also adds to its glamour. If a player loses all of his chips in a cash game, he can reach into his pocket and put more money on the table.

But if he loses all his chips in a tournament game, he is out of action and must head for the **rail**, the barrier that is placed between players and spectators. Nobody who plays serious poker likes being on the rail.

How Much Should You Bet in No-Limit Hold'em?

You don't have to decide how much you *should* bet in limit hold'em, you only need to know how much you *can* bet.

HOW TEXAS HOLD'EM IS PLAYED

Most limit hold'em players who decide to give no-limit hold'em a shot have to move outside their comfort zones and learn new betting skills. Deciding how much to bet or raise can pose quite a problem for new players.

Watching televised tournaments, it is sometimes hard to understand why players bet as many or as few chips as they do, but the truth is that most no-limit hold'em players follow a few simple guidelines that help them determine how much to bet. As a general rule, when you are the first person to enter the pot, you should raise three to four times the size of the big blind. Sometimes you might just call the minimum bet, and sometimes you might bet five or six times the size of the big blind.

In special circumstances you should bet all of your chips (move all in). We'll explain how much to bet in more detail in the section devoted to how to beat no-limit Texas hold'em.

Reading the Board Cards

You must be able to read the board so that you can determine what the best possible hand is as each community card is dealt. As each new board card hits the middle of the table, you should ask yourself, "What, at this moment, is the best possible hand?"

For example, if you start with two aces in your hand, you have the **nuts** before the flop, that is, the best possible hand at that moment.

You choose the best five-card poker hand by using any combination of your hole cards and the community cards. Your best hand can be any combination of none, one, or both of your cards combined with the cards in the middle. Look at it as having a seven-card hand, from which you choose the best five-card combination.

If a royal flush is dealt in the community cards, everybody playing the hand has a royal flush because that is the best hand possible. Or if the board cards come with K♠ Q♠ J♠ 10♠ and you have the A♠ in your hand, you have a royal flush and nobody else has one.

If you have two queens in your hand and a queen comes on the board, you have a **set**. If you have the A♣ K♣ and the J♣ 4♣ 8♥ come on the flop, you have the **nut flush draw**, that is, you are drawing to the best possible (nut) flush. Then if another club comes on the turn or river, you will make the nut flush. You also might flop a pair. Suppose the flop comes K♥ 6♣ 4♣ and you are holding the A♣ K♣. You would have top pair—two kings—with an ace kicker, and the nut flush draw, which would make you a very happy camper.

Depending on the cards that are dealt on the flop, the value of your hand may change. If you have two cards of the same suit in your hand and three cards in your suit come on the flop, you have made a flush, which probably is the best possible hand at the moment unless someone else has two cards in your suit, one of which is higher than your highest card.

But if the board pairs on the turn, your flush may no longer be the best hand because it is possible that someone else has made a full house. If the flop comes with the K♣ Q♦ 2♣ and you have the K♠ K♥

in your hand, you have the nuts on the flop. But what if another club comes on the turn?

One of your opponents could have a flush. Or another card (such as a 10) could be dealt that makes a straight for an opponent who has the A♦ J♥ in his hand. Either way, your three kings may no longer be the best hand.

Your Goals in the Game

We believe that your primary goal in playing Texas hold'em should be to enjoy yourself. Your second goal is winning money. Winning, of course, always adds to how much you enjoy playing the game.

In hold'em games, you win if all your opponents fold when you make a bet, or if you have the best hand at the showdown. In limit hold'em, more people play their cards all the way to the showdown than they do in no-limit hold'em, where hands seldom are played to the showdown.

You might also win by making a **bluff** bet. That is, you lead your opponents to believe that you have the best hand when you actually may not even have a pair. In limit hold'em, you can bluff by betting or raising the exact size of the maximum bet allowed. But in no-limit hold'em, you can bet any amount of chips you want up to the amount of chips you have sitting in front of you. Players often bluff in high-stakes televised no-limit hold'em tournaments, but bluffing isn't nearly as common in the everyday games that most of us play.

When you have mastered selecting the best hands to play, reading the board correctly, understanding the value of your hand, and determining when to hold'em and when to fold'em, you're on your way to beating Texas hold'em.

We'll look at the strategies now.

The Set-Up of a Hold'em Game

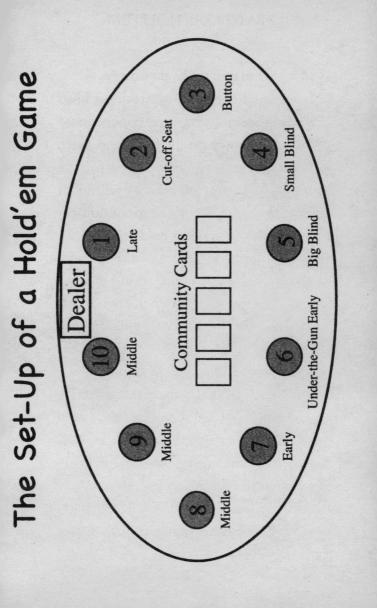

Limit Texas
Hold'em:
Everyone's
Favorite Game

Tom's Top 10
Winning Tips

1. ALWAYS PLAY GOOD
STARTING HANDS

What is a good Texas hold'em hand? Big cards are what bring home the most money in hold'em games. Aces, kings, queens, jacks—the **big pairs**—and A-K are the best starting hands, but how about some others? This is where your position in relation to the big blind starts to become more important. You can also play hands such as A-Q, A-J, pocket tens, pocket nines and pocket eights if you are sitting in a middle position and nobody has entered the pot in front of you.

The later your position the better, but in a game with a lot of **tight** players, players who play only premium hands and that are only infrequently in the pot, you might even raise with these hands if you are sitting in a middle or late position and you are the first player to enter the pot. Why? Because no one sitting in front of you has shown any strength.

But beware! Many hands that contain two face cards are not playable. A lot of otherwise playable hands go way down in value if a tight or solid player raises from an early position. For example, if that little old lady sitting in first position with a layer of dust on her chips suddenly raises, hands like A-Q, A-J and most pocket pairs are simply not playable. You must use good judgment in calling raises, even with strong starting hands.

How about connecting cards such as J-10, 9-8 or 7-6? In low-limit hold'em games, middle and low cards that connect to each other in rank—called **connectors**—can be very profitable hands in pots with three or more players, called **multiway** pots.

But here's the catch—you can play big pairs from any position at the table, but you should play middle or low connectors only from the last two or three positions on the button or one seat to the right of it.

This is good advice because connectors—suited or unsuited—play best in multiway pots, and you only know that the pot will be played multiway after you have found out whether the players sitting in front of you intend to play their hands. You can't know that information if you have to act early in the hand.

2. YOUR SEAT POSITION RELATIVE TO THE BUTTON STRONGLY INFLUENCES WHICH HANDS YOU PLAY

This is the most important concept in low-limit hold'em. The later your position, the more hands you can play and the more aggressive you can be. When you have a drawing hand, you will know how many opponents you have and how much it's going to cost to see the next card. None of this information is available if you are playing from an early position.

"Get it through your head that most hold'em players, even professional players, even world champions, lose vast sums of money from early positions for their entire poker playing careers!" Mike Caro wrote.

He believes that a strong argument can be made for playing only aces, kings, and A-K suited when you are sitting in early position in a 10-handed limit hold'em game if aggressive players are still to act after you. Caro is right—if you want to stop losing money in low-limit hold'em, play only your strongest hands in the first or second chair to the left of the big blind.

In a nutshell, tight is right in limit hold'em games, especially when you are sitting in an early position in the betting sequence.

Even from middle position you should have a fairly strong starting hand if you are the first or second player to enter the pot. Playing too many hands **out of position** (from a bad position in the betting sequence) is the most common mistake that new players make in limit hold'em games.

3. ALWAYS ASK YOURSELF FOUR QUESTIONS ON THE FLOP:

• What is the best possible hand?

• Am I holding it or do I have a draw to it?

• How likely is my opponent to be holding it?

• What is the probable strength of my opponents' cards?

You must be able to read the board cards correctly throughout the hand. You need to determine what the best possible hand on the flop could be and what are the most likely draws that could improve your hole cards or an opponent's cards to the nut hand on fourth street or fifth street. As each community card is placed face up on the table, decide what the best possible hand is.

The next question to ask yourself is how strong your hand is in relation to the flop. Do you have the nuts at the moment or a draw to it?

Most of the time you will neither have the nut hand nor face an opponent who is holding the nut hand. However, you still need to know what the best possible hand is and how likely it is that one of your opponents is holding it.

You are a detective and the betting actions of your opponents are clues to the probable strength of their hands. Try to determine their styles of betting as early as possible.

For example, does John usually bet a flush draw in late position, but never bets it when he is in the first or second seat after the blinds? Will Howard bet with **rags**, bad cards, on the button if everyone checks? Does Betty play "any-ace," an ace with a low kicker?

If Nate checks on the flop but calls your late position bet, ask yourself, "Self, what hand could he be drawing to?"

Beware slow-play artists who check-call the flop, check-call the turn, and then check-raise the river—they are usually holding the nut hand or something close to it, and are trying to suck you into their trap.

4. SOLID BASIC STRATEGY IS MORE IMPORTANT THAN PSYCHOLOGY IN LOW-LIMIT TEXAS HOLD'EM

Psychology can be very important in high-stakes hold'em games, but at the lower limits it is not nearly as crucial. Having a good basic strategy and knowing the starting hands to play from different positions at the table is far more important than trying to psyche out your opponents.

Knowing some of the simple math of poker—such as the number of outs (cards that will complete your hand) you have and your pot odds—is far more essential to your long-term success in the lower-limit games. You don't have to be a rocket scientist or a math genius to be successful.

Come to think of it, the only time I ever played with a rocket scientist at the poker table I found that he didn't have a good grasp of the fundamentals of the game and was a duck out of water. If your opponent doesn't know the relative strength of either his hand or your hand, fancy plays and psychological ploys will be wasted on him. Many novice low-limit hold'em players have a very simple philosophy—when in doubt, call!

5. DON'T DRAW TO A LOWER HAND WHEN A HIGHER HAND IS POSSIBLE

When there is a lot of action on the flop and turn, someone usually has either the nut hand or a draw to it. Sometimes they also **jam the pot**, raise and reraise, to make it expensive for you to draw to a better hand. You must always be careful that the hand you are drawing to will be the best hand if you make it.

Suppose you have a flush draw and the board pairs on fourth street. Someone could have made a full house or four of a kind. This means that even if you make your flush, you will lose. In other words, you are **drawing dead**. It is very expensive to make your hand only to find that it's a loser. And if the pot is jammed, you probably are a loser for sure.

Another common mistake is drawing to the **ignorant end**, the low end, of a straight.

For example, suppose you limped into the pot in late position with the 7-6 of spades. The flop comes 9-8-7 **rainbow** (three different suits). You have made a pair with a draw to a straight. Take another look at that board. What if a 10 comes off the deck on fourth street?

Aha! You have made your straight, but anyone who has a jack has made a bigger straight. You may have only three outs—the remaining three jacks in the deck—just to get a tie.

Even if you stay in the pot and hit a jack, you might find a player with a queen in his hand—and you still lose. Get the picture?

6. PLAY MORE CONSERVATIVELY IN GAMES WITH A LOW BRING-IN BET AND MOST JACKPOT GAMES

In many $4-$8 hold'em games in Las Vegas, the small blind is $1, the big blind is $2, and the pre-flop come-in bet is $2. With a $4 maximum wager on the flop and the $2 come-in bet at half that amount, these games have a low bring-in bet in relation to the maximum bet on the flop.

Because it is so cheap to see the flop, many low-limit players will enter more pots than they would if the come-in bet were $4 (a full bet instead of a half-bet).

The better strategy is to enter fewer pots, which means that you will be playing somewhat tighter than most of your opponents. Don't use the lower bring-in bet as an excuse to play more hands.

Some players will lower their starting requirements too much and start gambling with speculative hands more often than they should. This leads to financial loss. When you start playing too many hands, you have lowered your game to their level. Don't do it, not once, not ever.

In **jackpot games**—where a premium hand, such as aces-full or four-of-a-kind, pays out bonus money—there is usually an additional **rake** (money the casino takes out of pots to cover expenses) for the jackpot in addition to the standard rake.

If you enter more pots than optimal strategy dictates, your stack is paying for both of these extractions. Don't allow a mediocre jackpot to lure you into playing looser than you should.

Although I have seen many hold'em players **limp** (just call) in from an early position with small pairs and then call a

double raise behind them, this is simply too expensive *unless* the jackpot is huge. If the jackpot is gigantic, you are getting an **overlay** (good odds) on your investment and can justify seeing more flops.

Small pairs and suited connectors are the favorite starting hands of most jackpot players because winning the jackpot usually requires either aces-full or four-of-a-kind (or better) to be beaten by a better hand.

If you do decide to play in a jackpot game, be sure you understand all the rules and how much additional rake the casino is going to charge you.

7. SELDOM RAISE BEFORE THE FLOP

Unless you have a big pair such as aces, kings or queens, you are usually better off not raising before the flop in low-limit hold'em games. The reason is simple: Lots of players often call raises before the flop and whereas big pairs can sometimes win the pot without getting help from the board cards, almost all your other starting hands will need improvement in order to win.

Remember, even an A-K suited is still a drawing hand. When you have Big Slick, you will only flop a pair to it about 30 percent of the time, and will flop a flush draw only about 11 percent of the time.

I frequently see players jam the pot with A-K, flop nothing but **overcards**—cards that are of higher rank than the board—and still continue to play the hand, often calling raises after the flop. They sometimes even go to the river trying to snag an ace or king.

Sometimes they catch it and still lose; other times they miss and complain that the player who called several raises before the flop with 6-5 offsuit made two pair and beat them. Who played worse, the guy who flopped two pair and then started raising, or the player with the A-K who continued playing *after* the flop with only overcards?

Do most of your gambling after you see the flop, not before, unless you hold one of the three biggest pairs. That way you **can get away from** (fold) your hand cheaply if you don't flop anything good. And if you flop something you like, you can charge your opponents a heavy price to draw against you.

8. THE BLUFF IS HIGHLY OVERRATED IN LIMIT HOLD'EM

People get the idea that bluffing is a big part of limit hold'em because they've seen players bluff in no-limit hold'em tournaments on television. It is exciting to watch, but what may work in a no-limit hold'em game may not work in a small limit hold'em game.

Heed the advice tournament champion T.J. Cloutier and I wrote in *Championship Hold'em*: "All forms of *limit* poker are designed to have a showdown. Players frequently bluff in big-bet poker, in pot-limit and no-limit games.

"But remember in limit games, the pot may have 20 bets in it and it is only going to cost an opponent one more bet to call. He's going to make that call most of the time if he has any kind of hand at all. Therefore you simply cannot steal many pots by bluffing in limit hold'em."

Limit hold'em games are designed to have a showdown on the river. The pot is often so large that players with very marginal hands will call. They only have to call a single bet to try to win a pot that may already contain 15 or more bets.

Also, a "sheriff" usually is sitting at the table. The **sheriff** wants to keep everybody honest and thus will call your bet with marginal hands; he won't be able to sleep at night if he thinks he's been bluffed. These are two reasons why bluffing too often is a mistake in low-limit hold'em games.

When can you bluff? The three game conditions you are looking for when you attempt a bluff are:

1. When the pot is small;

2. When you have superior position over your opponents; and

3. When you are playing against only one or two opponents who play on the conservative side.

9. YOU USUALLY HAVE TO SHOW DOWN THE BEST HAND TO WIN A MULTIWAY POT IN LOW-LIMIT GAMES

You simply cannot win by bluffing at a multiway pot. Why? Because in hotly contested pots with three or four players, your opponents will rarely fold at the river because it costs only a single bet to call.

And oftentimes there will be more than one caller at the showdown. After all, if the pot is multiway and several players have stayed to the river, they must have some sort of hand, right?

Here's another way to think about a multiway pot: When several players already have invested lots of bets, the pot becomes what we call a **protected pot**. A single bet at the river will never induce anyone with even a remote chance of winning to fold for that final bet because the pot is "protected" from theft by its grandiose size. Even players with the second-best and third-best hands usually will call because they think their weaker hands may just be good enough to claim the pot.

Thus, you must have the best hand to win a multiway pot at the river—or at least a better hand than anyone else. But you can't steal a protected pot with a bluff-bet.

10. MAINTAIN YOUR DISCIPLINE

In low-limit Texas hold'em games, maintaining your discipline is the key to success. Avoiding the "tilt" factor will assist you in overcoming short-term bad luck, while helping ensure long-term success.

What exactly is the tilt factor? Going on **tilt** means that after a series of bad beats, an otherwise solid player suddenly starts playing a lot more hands—usually very marginal hands and often out of position. He lowers his starting hand requirements and starts chasing his losses.

Sometimes even top professional players go on tilt. When that happens, a game that would not be considered a playable game by most standards suddenly becomes a thing of beauty.

The best pros know enough about discipline and their own tilt factor to get up from the table and take a walk when things start to go bad. I would advise you to do the same.

I don't know of a player on the planet who, after suffering two or three bad beats in a row, can honestly say he is not somewhat emotionally upset over the way things are going.

Controlling our emotions is the key to success. How can we dominate our opponents if we're not in control of ourselves?

10 Practice Hands

Practice Hand # 1
Big Pairs (A-A and K-K)

Suppose you're **under the gun** (you're sitting in the first seat to the left of the big blind) in a cash game or tournament and you look down at the boss hand, **two aces**. It doesn't matter how many chips you have in front of you or what stage of the tournament you're playing, bring the pot in for a raise. Don't **limp** (just call) with two aces unless there is a maniac sitting behind you who raises every pot. In that case, since you know that he's going to raise the pot anyway, you might just call and then reraise if he raises.

Whether you're in first position, middle position or last position, raise with this hand. Why? To try to limit the field. You don't mind playing aces against one or two players, but you don't want to be forced to play against everybody at the table.

A pair of aces is the best hand that you can start with in limit hold'em and you want to win the pot without giving your opponents a free ride to beat you with inferior hands. If the opponents who called your bet or raise before the flop are reasonable players, lead at it on the flop *unless* big connected cards flop.

Play **pocket kings** about the same way you play pocket aces. Just be aware that if an ace hits the board on the flop, you have to back off. Suppose someone sitting in an early position has raised the pot and another player has called the raise before the flop. Reraise with your two kings. Make them pay to get a chance at catching a good flop with a weak ace, for example.

Of course, there are some inexperienced limit hold'em players who never lay down an "ace-anything" hand before the flop, but even though you might lose to them now and then, these are the kinds of players that you want to play against because you will beat them in the long run.

Try to get it heads-up with your pocket "cowboys." If you put in raise number two and your opponent puts in raise number three, you have to call him. There's a chance that you might be up against aces, but not necessarily. Watch your opponents. How aggressively do they play two jacks or small pairs? Do they put in a third bet with two queens? Let that information guide your betting decisions.

In summary, play two kings very aggressively before the flop and hope that an ace doesn't hit the board. Remember that when you're playing against only one or two players, a big pair has a good chance of holding up, but if you're playing against a lot of players, you can't be nearly as aggressive with it. This is why you always raise with your kings: You want to play the hand heads-up.

After the flop, you have to play pocket kings according to which cards come on the board. You face the same types of danger flops with pocket kings that you face with pocket aces, only more so because of the danger of an ace flopping. You're starting with the second-best hand in hold'em, but when you have kings, it sometimes seems like all the other cards in the deck are aces!

Practice Hand # 2
Big Pairs (Q-Q and J-J)

Pocket queens is a raising hand before the flop from any position in limit hold'em. And sometimes it is a reraising hand. Always keep in mind that there are two overcards to the queen that people play all the time in limit hold'em.

For example, suppose a solid player in seat one raises before the flop and another good player calls the raise before it gets to you. One or the other of them might have two aces, two kings, or an A-K. For that reason, just call with your pocket queens, don't reraise.

Now let's say that a player in the first seat next to the big blind has raised and a solid player in the second seat has reraised. You're sitting in the third seat with six players (including the two blinds) waiting to act after you. What do you do?

Usually, you fold. Although you've picked up a strong hand, you don't have any money involved in the pot, and since it's been raised and reraised before you've even had a chance to act, it's easy to just throw them away.

So what if the guy in the first seat only has two tens? The player next to him might have two aces or two kings or A-K. Why take a chance of losing money against such heavy betting when you can get a new hand to play in about two minutes?

Pocket jacks is a hand that you can play from any position at the table when you are the *first* player to enter the pot. Bring it in for a raise, but if you get reraised, just call. After you see the flop, you can decide whether to continue with the hand.

Now suppose you're in late position and a couple of players have limped in front of you. You still raise the pot. Why?

To try to get everyone sitting behind you, including the blinds, to fold.

Another reason to raise is to build the pot. The factor that determines the value of your pocket jacks is the number of people playing the hand with you. The more players in the pot, the more vulnerable you are. Heads-up, two jacks is a big, big hand.

If you're sitting one seat in front of the button or on the button, raise with pocket jacks if the pot hasn't been raised yet. Your raise might knock out the people between you and the first bettor. If someone reraises, just flat-call. If you get unlucky and an ace, king or queen flops, you can always fold the hand. But if the flop comes with a jack in it, bingo!

But when it comes with overcards and you have two or more opponents, there's a pretty good chance that you're beaten, so you say adios to your "hooks" and send them into the muck if anyone bets.

Practice Hand # 3
Big Connecting Cards (A-K and A-Q)

From almost any position, you can raise with **A-K**. And if you've been watching your opponents, you might even **reraise** against most of them.

You can raise from the blinds but usually, do not reraise because you will have to act first from the flop on, which puts you out of position.

If you're sitting in a late position and somebody has raised in front of you, reraise with an A-K. You will have them on the defensive because they will have to act first after the flop.

If you're in the first three positions, bring it in for a raise. If you're in fourth, fifth, sixth or seventh position, you can reraise with A-K. And again, if you're in the small or big blind, the most you should do is raise with the hand, you should not reraise with it.

Many of today's limit hold'em players play A-K, or ace-anything in fact, like it's the total nuts. A lot of players raise with A-Q, A-J, A-10 and even A-9 because they love playing any suited ace.

You're a big favorite over these types of hands when you have an A-K—and that is why you always reraise with it if anyone raises in front of you, meaning that you will not have to act first after the flop.

You might lose a few pots against opponents with weaker aces, but in the long run you're going to win a lot more often than you lose because you started with the best hand.

An **A-Q** is a good hand in limit hold'em because so many people these days are playing small connectors and lesser holdings that are not as strong as an A-Q. You can raise with A-Q from any position to try to limit the field, just as you do with A-K, but don't usually reraise with it. If the flop comes ace-high or queen-high, you have a pretty good hand.

When the flop comes queen high, you have top pair-top kicker; and when it comes ace-high, you have top pair with second-best kicker. You would like to be up against a K-Q or Q-J when the flop comes queen-high because then you're sitting in clover with a better kicker.

There are a few situations in a tournament, however, when you might reraise with an A-Q. Suppose you're sitting on the button and a player who has only enough chips for one more bet raises the pot.

In this case, reraise to put him all in. By raising him all-in, you're not going to get blown out on the flop if it doesn't come with anything that helps you—and hopefully, you will knock him out of action.

Another situation where you can reraise with A-Q is when you're in very late position and an aggressive player sitting to your immediate right raises. You reraise in this spot because you probably have the best hand, plus you will get to act after he acts on the flop.

Practice Hand # 4
Medium Connectors (J-10 and 8-7)

You don't want to give a J-10 too much credit because it has definite liabilities. You can play it, of course, but J-10 is a hand that you must play very carefully under the right conditions.

Some of the right conditions include scenarios where you are in a late position in a multiway and unraised pot, and when you are defending the big blind for a single bet.

In a raised pot, you usually fold with J-10. A lot of players who believe that J-10 is a super hand, suited or unsuited, forget that even a lowly Q-6 offsuit has a higher card in it than a J-10. And if you flop either a jack or a 10 as top pair, you don't have a good kicker, do you?

If the pot has been raised and called before it gets to you, you are a definite underdog in the hand with only a J-10, suited or unsuited. Being suited does not increase its value enough to justify calling a raise. Even if the pot is raised and nobody else calls between you and the raiser, your J-10 is still a dog.

The real strength of J-10 is the 10. A straight cannot be made without a ten or a five, so the power of J-10 is the multitude of straights that you can make with it. You can flop a lot of different made straights to this hand, and you can flop a lot of straight draws with it.

In tournaments, J-10 is the type of hand that can cost you all of your money. Suppose you call a bet before the flop and you flop some possibilities. You call another bet on the flop, and you don't make your draw on fourth street. Now you have to decide whether to continue.

You might think, "I've already lost two bets before the flop and a bet on the flop. Now it's going to cost me a double bet on the turn. But I've got so much money in the pot already, I'm gonna continue." That's the dilemma that hands like J-10 can put you in.

Our advice: Fold. Take your loss and move on to the next hand.

Hands such as **8-7 suited** are virtually unplayable in early to middle position. If you're in late position and a few limpers are in the pot, that's a different story—now you have position. You need to have at least two callers in front of you to play the hand, even when you're next to the button or on the button.

You have to get a perfect flop to a hand that's only eight-high, otherwise you can lose a lot of chips. For that reason, it just isn't a hand that you usually want to play in a tournament.

The hands that you really want to play in tournament poker are the ones that you *don't* have to get a perfect flop to—and that's one of the big differences between tournament play and cash-game play.

Practice Hand # 5
Medium Pairs (10-10 and 9-9)

Pocket tens is a very playable hand in a lot of limit hold'em situations—but it isn't playable at all in other situations. For example, you usually should pass if solid players sitting in early positions have bet, raised and reraised before the flop.

However, if everybody else comes into the pot and you're getting a huge price for calling the double or triple bet, you might call. Just keep in mind that you probably need to flop a set to stay in the hand. With two tens, you're the "favorite" to see one or more overcards hit the board

Pocket tens have the best chance of holding up against one or two opponents. If the pot is played multiway, you almost always have to flop a set or make a lucky straight on the turn or river to win the pot. In fact the only advantage two tens have over some of the other pairs is a 10 because either a 10 or a 5 is always necessary to make a straight.

If you're in early position, you can bring it in for a raise. When you're in middle position and three or four people have passed in front of you, automatically raise.

If one or two players have limped into the pot, usually just flat-call to try to see the flop cheaply. If you are playing in a super loose game where everybody is playing a lot of hands, you might want to just call with pocket tens from early position to mix up your play a little bit in the hope of flopping a set. You limp in because you are expecting to get multiway action, and because players at these loose tables don't usually respect early-position raises.

If you are sitting in a late position and someone who is sitting to your right in middle to late position brings it in for a raise, you generally want to reraise to try to isolate and get the action heads up.

Your equity goes up because if you can drive everybody else out of the pot, you probably have the best starting hand, and you will have position on the raiser. If he reraises, just flat-call and make a decision after you see the flop.

Obviously, if you flop a 10 you have a powerful hand. Your main concern then becomes deciding how to extract the most money you can from your opponent. Usually the later the position that the initial raise comes from, the less strength the raiser needs to bring it in for a raise.

Pocket nines can be a very tricky hand to play. It's a little too good to throw away, but it's also very vulnerable in an early position. Nines, tens and jacks are in about the same category. A pair of jacks is about 50-50 to catch one or more overcards on the flop, and a pair of nines is weaker of course. In early position you might just limp in with pocket nines because you want to see the flop cheaply.

Suppose you're on the button with pocket nines and one or two people have limped into the pot. You usually would just call because if you raise, the limpers probably are going to call the single raise—and the types of hands that they often limp with are the connecting cards such as Q-J or J-10, overcards to your nines.

But you might also raise. Raising will cost you only one extra bet; you know that most or all the limpers are going to call you, and your raise will build the pot. You are hoping to flop a set and win a decent pot with the nines, realizing you can fold them if overcards hit the board on the flop.

If just one overcard hits the board and everybody checks, you can bet. But what if the flop comes with two overcards? In that case, the limpers often will check to the raiser, and therefore give you a chance at a free card by also checking.

A big mistake that people make in hold'em is betting after all their opponents have checked to them when the flop comes with two or more overcards. Why not take the free card? If you bet and someone check-raises, you will have to fold the hand immediately and will wind up losing a bet when it didn't have to cost you anything to see one more card.

Practice Hand # 6
Small Pairs (8-8 and Lower)

Pocket eights or sevens usually are not hands that you want to play unless the pot will be played with a big field, in which case you don't mind gambling with the small pairs in the hope of flopping a set.

Naturally this means that you are sitting in a late table position, because otherwise you cannot be sure that the pot will be played multiway. In other words, you can play small pairs from late position for the minimum bet when there are several callers in front of you.

What should you do if you limp into the pot with a small pair and someone raises behind you? You can call one more bet, but if an opponent raises behind you and another player reraises, the proper play usually is to fold. If you are playing against conservative players and no one has entered the pot, you can even raise from late position with a small pocket pair.

Just remember that you must be the first player to enter the pot with only one or two players who can act after you bet. Don't try this play if most of your opponents are loose players because they usually will call you with any ace or any suited high card-low card combination.

Although a **pair of fives** is a small pair it has an added value: A five or a 10 is always needed to make a straight. If you catch a flop such as 4-3-2, which gives you an open-end straight draw and an overpair, you're in clover.

If you're lucky enough to catch an ace on the turn, and one of your opponents is holding an ace, you've beaten him with your straight.

Of course, it's a little bit dangerous if a five hits on the turn to give you a set because, unfortunately, the player with the ace has made the straight! You don't necessarily have to fold in this scenario, just play the hand cautiously.

Always keep in mind that limit hold'em is a big-card game. If you play small pairs from an early position, you always take the risk of losing your money. You must hit a set or get some other fantastic flop to win with these little pairs. (Sets will win 80 percent or more of the time when you flop one.)

The best strategy for playing sixes or lower when you are dealt them in the first three or four seats is to throw them away, especially in a tournament. People play a lot more hands in cash games because the pots are multiway far more often than they are in tournaments, and they play a lot of small pairs in the hope of flopping a set and winning a monster pot. There's nothing wrong with that, but don't do it in a tournament because small pairs usually will just burn up your money.

Practice Hand # 7
Small Connectors (5-4)

The higher your connectors, the better off you are. Small suited connectors, of course, are not as strong as the middle suited connectors because many times they make the weak end of the straight. If you have a 5-4 suited the only time that you can make the nut straight is when A-2-3,

2-3-6, or 3-6-7 are on the board. If the flop comes 8-7-6 you can be in a world of hurt with the "idiot" end of the straight.

A flush is not what you are hoping to make if your small connectors are suited. For example, suppose you flop a flush. Any player who has a single higher card in your suit can make a bigger flush on the turn or river if a fourth suited card hits the board, and most of them will call on the flop to see fourth street. If the fourth flush card comes on fourth street, you have to be very careful in deciding whether you wish to continue with the hand.

You can play this type of hand when you are in the small blind and it costs you only one-half a bet more to see the flop. You also might defend the big blind with small connectors in a multiway pot.

Or you may play it for a single bet on the button when at least two other people already are in the pot and you don't think that either of the blinds will raise.

Practice Hand # 8
"Any-Ace" suited

An ace suited or offsuit with a card lower than a 10 is what we call an "any-ace" hand. In loose cash games you'll see a lot of people playing "any-ace," particularly if the ace is suited. These types of players play very aggressively, usually overbetting their hands and giving a lot of loose action.

Any-ace suited is a weak hand, although there are a few situations in which you might play it. For example, you can call with any-ace from the small blind for half a bet if the pot has not been raised.

You also might call with this type of hand when you're on or next to the button in an unraised pot and several players already are in the pot. In this case you figure that the ace might be good because if someone else had a big ace, he probably would have raised. And if everyone has passed to you on the button, you can raise with an any-ace hand to attack the blinds.

Just remember that if several people have limped into the pot and you call on the button with a hand such as the A♠ 6♠, you're not looking to win with a lone ace. If you happen to win with the ace by itself, lucky you—but what you're really hoping for on the flop is two sixes, an ace and a six, or three spades.

Practice Hand # 9
One-Gap Hands (Q-10)

Connected cards that aren't connected to the next-lowest card are called one-gap hands, two-gap hands, or three-gap hands depending on the number of missing ranks between the high and low card. Q-10 is an example of a one-gap hand people often play in low-limit hold'em games.

Being suited always makes a hand more valuable, but whether suited or unsuited, Q-10 is a hand that requires a lot of skill to play properly, especially in tournaments. It is what we call a "trouble hand" that you can play primarily from a late table position when the pot has not been raised.

From early position, fold this trouble hand. If you just call from an early position and an opponent reraises, the hand goes way down in value, which is one reason why Q-10 is awkward to play in the first three seats to the left of the big blind.

For example, suppose you call with Q-10, the action is raised behind you, and you call the raise. If you flop a pair to the hand, you cannot know for certain whether you have the best kicker.

Many people play Q-Q, Q-J, K-Q, A-Q, so when you flop a queen to your Q-10, you're likely to have a big kicker problem.

And you're out of position in the betting sequence since you will have to make a betting decision before the players who are sitting behind you.

If you are sitting in the cutoff seat (one place to the right of the button) or on the button, you might call from late position with Q-10 but you generally would not raise with it. However if nobody else has entered the pot, you might raise with Q-10 to try to get heads-up with the blinds.

Q-10 is an especially troublesome hand in tournaments because you can't buy more chips if you lose the pot. Suppose the flop comes with Q-J-4, which is an extremely dangerous board when you have a Q-10. Although you have flopped top pair, you have a weak kicker. And if you hit a 10 on the turn to make two pair, the 10 would make a straight for anyone who has an A-K or a K-9.

Furthermore, someone may already have queens and jacks or even a set of fours. You may even get a good flop for your hand and still have to fold it.

Suppose the flop comes Q-9-7. If someone bets and another player raises before it's your turn to act, you must fold because the chances are slim to zero that you have the best hand.

So what kind of flop do you want? You'd much rather see a 10 on the flop than a queen because your queen would be a decent kicker for the 10. What you're really hoping to make is two pair, trips, or a lucky straight. Therefore your ideal flops would be Q-10-2, 10-10-3, or A-K-J.

Practice Hand # 10
Two-Gap Hands (K-10)
With this two-gapper, in which you're missing the Q-J, you have to be very careful to select just the right circumstances in

which you play your K-10. For example, in a limit hold'em tournament, you might play K-10 when you are in late position and nobody else has entered the pot.

In this situation, K-10 is a reasonable hand with which to attack the blinds by raising, but only if they are conservative players who are likely to fold against your raise. And in a cash game you can call when you are sitting on the button and one or more players have already entered the pot for the minimum bet.

Be forewarned, however, that this two-gap hand can spell trouble any time that you play it in a raised pot. Against a solid player who raises from up front, fold a K-10 even if you are in the big blind and no one else has called the raise.

If several people have called the raise, you might consider playing the hand if it is suited. Ask yourself, "If Solid Sam has raised from early position and several people have called him, what could they be calling with?" They could easily be holding K-Q, A-10, K-J, or better. In that case, if you don't catch a lucky straight or two pair to your K-10, you probably are beaten.

Now suppose you are in the big blind with a K-10 and an action player raises from the button. In this situation, you can call the extra bet to see the flop.

And if you are the small blind and only one other player has entered the pot for the minimum bet, you can call for one-half a bet to see what comes on the flop.

What if you have K-10 in the small blind and nobody else is in the pot, meaning that you can play the hand head-up against the big blind? In this scenario, you can raise with K-10 to try to win the blinds.

Always remember that K-10 has more value if the pot has not been raised. What do people normally raise with? Big pairs and high cards with big kickers. That is why you play K-10 only when you are sitting in a late position and the pot has not been raised.

Because people limp in with hands such as K-Q, K-J and A-10, you still have to be cautious even if you flop top pair.

Suppose the flop comes K-8-4. If someone bets from early position into a field of four or five people, you don't like your pair of kings a whole lot because there's a good chance that the bettor has a higher kicker.

You would much rather see a flop such as 10-5-2 because your king is the second-best kicker possible. You just hope that nobody has an A-10!

Shane's Review Questions

1. What is the best betting position at the table?

The button. The more players who have to act before you must act, the more information you can collect about the strength of their cards, and the more options you have in deciding how to best play your hand.

2. Why is playing solid basic strategy more important than trying to make crafty plays in low-limit poker?

Because most low-limit players, especially beginners, just play their cards without paying much attention to how their opponents play. Fancy moves and strategic raises work far better against experienced players than against new players.

3. Why can you play more hands with medium connectors in limit hold'em than in no-limit hold'em?

Far more pots are played multiway in limit hold'em than in no-limit hold'em. The more people in the pot, the more profitable it is to play medium connectors such as 10-9 and 8-7, which need three other people in the pot to get proper odds. Thus, limit hold'em is the better game in which to play them.

4. Why should you usually play medium connectors from a late position only?

Because when you enter a pot from an early position, you cannot predict whether the pot will be played multiway. But when you are sitting in a late position, you know how many players already have entered the pot and can thus determine whether the pot will have enough players to give you the best chance of winning with your connecting cards.

5. Why do you usually have to show down the best hand on the river to win a multiway pot in low-limit hold'em games?

Because there is so much money at stake in multiway pots that even players who have the second-best or even the third-best hands often will call on the river. After all, it usually costs only one bet to gamble that you can win a pot that may have 20 bets in it.

6. Why should you bluff less often in limit hold'em than you do in no-limit hold'em?

In no-limit hold'em, you can make a huge raise that is so big that nobody dare call it, even if they think you might be bluffing. But in limit hold'em, you can bet or raise only the size of the big blind – and hardly anyone will fold for a single bet when there are lots of bets already in the pot.

7. Why is it important to watch how your opponents play, even when you aren't playing a hand?

So that you can better predict what they are likely to do when you *are* playing a hand against them. By studying the kinds of hands they show down on the river, you can learn a lot about their starting hand requirements. And by noticing whether they usually will call a raise when they are in the big blind, you can better determine whether to raise their big blind when you are sitting on the button.

The more you know about what your opponents are likely to do in certain situations, the better your chances of outplaying them and winning the money. And the more money you win, the more you enjoy playing hold'em, right?

How Would You Play This Hand?

ACE-KING IN A LOW-LIMIT HOLD'EM CASH GAME

I recently received an e-mail from Stanley, who has been having some difficulty in the play of A-K in both tournaments and cash games. In a $3-$6 limit hold'em game at a casino in Las Vegas, he held A-K in a middle position. A player sitting one seat to the left of the big blind raised the pot and one other player called.

114

"I hesitated momentarily to decide whether I should call, fold, or reraise," he wrote. "I noticed that the raiser previously had raised with pocket nines."

How Would You Play This Hand?
a. Fold
b. Call
c. Reraise

Here's How Stanley Played It

"I decided to just call. In retrospect, I think I should have folded. An ace came on the flop, the raiser bet, and I raised to knock out the man on my left, who then folded. The raiser just called rather than reraising me. On the turn he checked.

I should have checked behind him because he check-raised me. I called the raise and on the river, he bet and I called. He showed pocket aces to beat my A-K.

"My question is this: Against a raise from a player in early position, should I usually fold when I hold A-K?"

Tom's Analysis of Stanley's Play

Big Slick, as we fondly refer to A-K, is one of the premium hands in limit, pot-limit, and no-limit hold'em. It also is perhaps the trickiest and most difficult one to play correctly. Thinking that maybe he should have folded his A-K against the early-position raiser, Stanley is second-guessing himself because he got a bad result when he ran into pocket aces and got massacred.

But he has overlooked one little thing that I have taught many of my students: You are rewarded for correct play in the long run; in the short run, anything can happen.

If you are routinely in the habit of folding A-K in limit hold'em against an early-position raiser, you're playing way too tight and have very little chance of being able to beat the game. A-K is not a "made" hand; a big pair is a "made" hand. A-K is a drawing hand, which means that if you don't flop something to it, most of the time you should simply give up after the flop. But if you do flop something to your A-K, you usually will have top pair with top kicker or, occasionally, a lucky straight. With top pair and top kicker, you should be fairly aggressive unless you have reason to believe that there is greater strength out against you.

In Stanley's situation where the flop came with an ace in it, he certainly had a hand that was worth at least one raise. When he got check-raised, he correctly put on the brakes and just called his opponent down.

I would have played the hand the same way; I certainly wouldn't have thought that I had made a mistake in my play of the hand. Unless the early-position raiser is a notorious rock that never raises with anything less than a big pair and would never check-raise unless he had one pair beaten, I certainly would have to call down the raiser and pay him off.

If you're in the habit of laying down top pair with top kicker, you're going to have problems in any hold'em game. The point is that you cannot judge the correctness of your play by results alone. You must go by what you know to be the correct play.

A TWO-GAP HAND IN A $3-$6 CASH GAME

Now comes another question that evolves around Big Slick, this time from a player who highly suspected that he was up against the dangerous duo in a ring game. John, the reader who e-mailed me this scenario, is "slightly more than a rank beginner" at hold'em and is "trying hard to learn some of the finer points of the game."

He was playing in a $3-$6 hold'em game when a situation arose in which he thinks that he may have made two errors, one of which he believes may have been misplaying his hand at the river.

"The game was nine-handed and I was in seventh position," he began. "The player sitting two seats to the left of the big blind raised it to $6 before the flop. He is a retired man who plays a conservative and usually unimaginative game. I had a K-10 offsuit."

How Would You Play This Hand Before the Flop?

    a. Fold

    b. Call

    c. Raise

Here's How John Played It

"I called with my K-10 offsuit, and the button and the big blind both called behind me. The flop came 8-8-7 in three suits and everybody checked.

A deuce came on the turn and again it was checked around. At the river came a king, giving me kings and eights. The big blind checked and the original raiser bet. What was my correct play?"

How Would You Play This Hand on the River?

    a. Fold

    b. Call

    c. Raise

Here's How John Played It

"I don't know what the winning hand was for sure, because I decided that the bettor probably had an A-K and had me out-kicked, so I folded and so did the other two players. I thought that my play was correct, but the card room manager, a very good player, almost fell off his seat as he kibitzed me."

Tom's Analysis of John's Play

John, I agree that you made two errors in the play of the hand. Your first mistake was calling a raise with K-10. If the raiser is as conservative as you described him, he probably raised with a much better starting hand than yours. Why call with a K-10 if you think you're up against an A-K?

After you elected to take the free cards on the flop and turn, and after you finally paired at the river, I believe that since you already were in the pot, you should have called the final bet. Although you may not have liked doing it because you suspected that the bettor had a better kicker, the pot probably was laying you a big enough price (because of the pre-flop action) to make the call. Why call a pre-flop raise with a marginal hand, get there with it, and then fold for a single bet?!

But let me give you credit for one admirable trait, John: You're trying to learn the finer points of the game and are taking steps to get better at it. Keep analyzing your play and asking experienced players for their advice, and continue to read and study the material in good books, and these types of mistakes will soon disappear from your game. As soon as they do, I hope to see you in the winner's circle.

No Limit Hold'em: The Television Game

Tom's Top 10 Winning Tips

1. BIG PAIRS AND HIGH CARDS ARE THE BOSS HANDS IN NO-LIMIT HOLD'EM

No-limit hold'em is a game of big cards. Playing small pairs and medium suited connectors – unless you can play them cheaply from late position – is simply too expensive. The five best starting hands are aces, kings, queens, A-K and jacks. You usually can play these hands for a raise from any position.

Just remember that A-K, even suited, is still a drawing hand, not a made hand. You will usually have to flop something to A-K to make it profitable to continue playing after the flop.

Any pair lower than aces can get you into trouble before the flop if you don't play it properly. If someone is willing to put a lot of money in the pot before the flop, even a high pair could be in trouble.

If nobody has entered the pot and I am sitting on the button or right in front it, I will usually raise with any hand that has two cards 10 or higher in it.

This means that hands like J-10, Q-10, A-J, A-10, K-J, K-Q, K-10, A-Q and pocket tens become raising hands from a late position. (Naturally, the top five starting hands are also raising hands.) If someone re-raises me, I will have to decide whether to continue playing or fold.

When a player calls a raise with a suited ace with a small kicker such as A-5, for example, he can be up against a hand that also contains an ace with a bigger kicker. When this happens, the player with the A-5 is dominated by the ace-big kicker, and has only three outs (three ways to make a better hand) – the three remaining fives.

Of course, a draw to a flush or a straight could also develop, but that is not what happens most of the time. The point is that you should not call raises with this type of hand.

2. PLAY FEWER HANDS THAN YOU WOULD PLAY IN LIMIT HOLD'EM

To be a successful no-limit hold'em player you don't need to play a lot of hands, but you do need to win the majority of the hands you decide to play. Many hands that play reasonably well in limit hold'em—

hands such as A-Q, K-J suited, pocket tens and suited connectors in multiway pots—do not play nearly as well in no-limit hold'em.

The reason that these marginal hands don't do very well in no-limit hold'em is because your opponent can make a big enough bet to make it unprofitable to continue playing the hand.

In limit hold'em, where you and your opponents are restricted to a limited number of fixed bets and raises, you usually do not have to put your entire stack of chips in jeopardy on any one hand. This is not the case in no-limit hold'em, a game in which you can lose your entire stack on one bet.

Because you can lose all your chips on one hand, cards like the A-Q and K-J that I mentioned can be extremely troublesome and difficult to play in no-limit hold'em.

For example, suppose a player raises in early position and you are on the button with A-Q. You think to yourself, "Self, I have two big cards and position on this raiser. I'll call him and see what develops." The flop comes with A-10-5 **rainbow** (three different suits). Now you say to yourself, "Look, Self, I have top pair with a pretty good kicker. Yummy!"

Your opponent, the one who raised in early position, checks to you. "Well, Self, let's make about a pot-sized bet here," you think. "I probably have the best hand, so I might as well make a bet and try to win some more of my opponent's money."

You make the bet and your opponent studies you for a moment, staring at you intensely. Then he makes the exact announcement you didn't want to hear: "I'm raising you all in!" Now what do you do?

You're probably drawing to just three outs to win the pot, the three queens that are left in the deck. If you had been studying your opponent and had determined that he was a tight player, you probably should have folded your hand before the flop against his early-position raise.

This is just one example of the problems that can develop in the play of no-limit hold'em if you try to play the same types of hands you are accustomed to playing in limit hold'em.

Where only a few extra bets could be in jeopardy when you play a mediocre hand in limit hold'em, your entire stack of chips can be ruined when you play marginal cards in no-limit hold'em.

3. LEARN HOW MUCH TO RAISE

One of the most common mistakes that new players make in no-limit hold'em is betting the wrong amount of chips when they raise. New players usually do one of two things—they either underbet the pot or they overbet it. Either of these mistakes can get you into trouble.

Underbetting the pot is a very common mistake that beginning hold'em players make. Often times I see several people enter the pot for the minimum bet, which is always the size of the big blind. Then someone in late position makes a raise exactly double the size of the big blind, which is a very weak play.

Raising such a small amount won't drive any of the original callers out of the pot, and could give one of the early limpers an opportunity to make a much bigger raise, forcing everyone out of the pot. Why not try this tactic: simply call and see what develops after the flop? Having late position gives you the advantage on all future betting rounds.

Overbetting the pot is another common mistake. Suppose the blinds are $10-$25 and nobody has entered the pot yet. You look down and find two beautiful aces, the best possible starting hand. You get excited, your heart starts beating faster and you announce, "I raise!" as you shove $500 into the pot. Everyone folds, including the blinds, and you have just won the pot.

Winning the pot is good, of course, except for one minor detail—you have only made a $35 profit with the best possible starting hand. What happened?

You made the mistake of overbetting the pot and forcing everyone out. If you had bet a little less—around $100—you might have gotten a caller and won a bigger pot.

It's true that you could also have gotten outdrawn and lost with your aces, but that's a chance you must take. After all, you can't make an omelet without breaking a few eggs, and you can't be a winner at no-limit hold'em unless you can make the most profit out of your strong starting hands.

So, how much should you raise when you enter the pot in no-limit hold'em? As a general guideline, raise three to four times the size of the big blind. For example, if the big blind is $20, raise to $60 or $80.

4. PLAY VERY FEW HANDS WHEN YOU ARE SITTING IN EARLY POSITION

The earlier your position in relation to the big blind, the worse it is for you. The later your position, the better it is for you. Why? It is very simple.

When you are the last player to act, you know what everybody is doing before the action gets to you. This is a big advantage. If you are the first to act, all the other players have an edge on you because you have to act on your hand before they do. This means that many hands that are playable in late position are not playable in early position.

If you enter the pot from early position with the 10-9 of clubs, for example, you don't know whether someone will raise after you enter the pot. This could make that type of hand too expensive to play for profit. Hands with middle-rank connecting cards need lots of callers and, preferably, no pre-flop raise to make them worthwhile to play.

In a nutshell, the earlier you have to act the less information you have, and the later you have to act, the more information you have.

Most players, even professional players, lose money by playing hands in the first two seats after the big blind. Only the best starting hands like big pairs and A-

K can be played for a long-term profit from early position. Small pairs and suited connectors just do not play well from an early position.

5. GET TO KNOW THE PLAYING STYLES OF YOUR OPPONENTS AS SOON AS POSSIBLE

Poker is a people game played with cards, not a card game played with people. This means that you need to learn how to play your cards against the different types of opponents you are likely to face at the poker table. You should always try to play your hand one way against a tight conservative player, and play your hand in a completely different way against a loose aggressive player.

For example, say that you have the A-J of clubs and are sitting on the button. Tight Ted, who has not played a hand in over an hour, suddenly raises from an early position. What kind of hand do you think he has? By his previous play, he has showed you that he doesn't play very many hands. Now he has cards he likes enough to raise with from an early position. What should you do?

I know what I would do—I'd fold my hand in a New York minute against this type of player in this situation. I would be afraid that I was up against a big pair or A-K, which would make it very difficult for me to win the pot.

Now let's say that you have the same hand and again you are the button. Everybody folds to the player on your immediate right (the cut-off seat) and he raises. In fact Rammin' Robert has raised the last three hands in a row and has played over 50 percent of the hands dealt to him. What do you think of his raise and what should you do?

136

Again, I know what I would do against Robert—I'd reraise him. I probably have not only a better starting hand, I also have position on him. By reraising him I can probably force the blinds to throw their hands away, an added bonus for raising, and get it heads-up between the raiser and me.

The point is that against the tight player, I would fold, but against the loose player, I would raise.

In other words I would play the very same hand totally differently depending upon the playing style of my opponent. Learning the playing styles of all your opponents will accelerate your success at the poker table.

6. LEARN HOW TO BLUFF IN THE RIGHT SITUATIONS

The bluff is a major element in playing no-limit hold'em successfully. However many new players make the classic mistake of bluffing too often, probably because they've been watching too much "television poker."

The World Poker Tour on the Travel Channel and the World Series of Poker on ESPN bring all the top poker action right into your living room. What you are watching, however, is usually just the final-table action, not the play that allowed the finalists to get there.

When the audience sees players raising each other with hands like 4-3, or moving all their chips into the center of the table with nothing but a flush draw, they think that's how to play the game.

In other words, the audience is led to believe that players bluff far more often in no-limit hold'em that they actually do. The truth is that final-table action is quite a bit different from the play in the early stages of the tournament. Players have less reason to bluff in the opening rounds of the tournament because the blinds are much smaller and, therefore, they can afford to wait for strong starting hands. But at the final table, it's a different story because the blinds are very high – it simply costs too much to just sit and wait for a powerful hand.

Therefore, the players must try to maneuver each other out of the pot just to survive. This means that they sometimes attack each other with much weaker hands.

The bottom line is that what might be a correct bluffing situation in the final stages of the tournament could get you broke in the earlier stages.

Timing is everything in executing a successful bluff. That is why getting to know your opponents is so important.

Tighter players will often surrender their blinds without much of a fight. These players are easier to bluff.

Loose players who frequently defend their blinds and play lots of pots are much harder to bluff. They will gamble with you. Know your man, get your hand, and then bluff!

7. DON'T GET MARRIED TO A HAND

One of the most common mistakes that new players make is not folding a great starting hand that has been drawn out on. This usually happens when a player who started with a big pair such as aces or kings has raised before the flop and bet again on the flop. Then a straight card or a flush card comes on fourth street.

An opponent makes a big bet at the pot or even check-raises – and yet the pre-flop raiser continues playing the hand when it obviously is beaten. Here's the message: You must be able to fold a great hand once in a while to preserve your precious stack of chips. It doesn't matter if your opponent started with a much weaker hand than yours—if you're beaten, you must fold.

Another great hand that often goes awry is a pocket pair to which you flopped a set. A set will win around 80 percent of the time, a very high percentage indeed.

However if your set gets drawn out on, it can become very expensive unless you have the discipline to fold your hand and avoid getting broke to it. Suppose you start with pocket sevens and the flop comes K-Q-7 with two diamonds. With a flop like that, there could be both flush and straight draws out against you.

Now the turn card comes and a four of clubs hits the board. You bet again and still get called. The river card is the jack of diamonds, making both a possible flush and a possible straight. An opponent, known for his tight play, moves a mountain of chips to the center of the pot. What could he have?

Judging from the way he played the hand, he almost certainly has a flush, probably the nut flush. If he made a straight, and didn't believe you were playing a flush draw since you bet twice instead of just checking to get a free card, he would probably bet a straight also. Either way you're beaten. Therefore you must fold to preserve your chips.

8. RAISE MORE OFTEN THAN YOU CALL

No-limit hold'em is a bettor's game not a caller's game. Anytime you make a bet, especially a large bet, you are putting your opponent to a test. Anytime your opponent makes a big bet at you, he is putting you to a test. It is much better to be the tester than the tested.

In other words, you want to be the one who forces your opponent to guess what you have and make a decision based on speculation rather than the other way around. Most of the time he will guess wrong.

Many times you are faced with the decision to call another player's bet, fold to his bet, or raise. Of these three options, calling is usually the worst.

Many times it is a choice between folding or raising—and raising often is the best option. Players frequently raise with less than premium starting hands, but when faced with a reraise from a solid player like you, they will fold.

Callers usually are losers in no-limit hold'em. Does that mean you always either raise or fold? Of course not. There are times when I suspect that my opponent may be bluffing and therefore I will simply call him down.

If I'm wrong and he does have a strong hand, I will save money by not raising. If he is bluffing, he can't call my raise anyway, so a call is the best play.

Hey, nobody ever promised that this game was going to be easy.

9. PLAY GOOD TOURNAMENT STRATEGY, EVEN IN CASH GAMES

Tournament strategy is quite a bit different than cash game strategy. (Read the chapter on tournaments to learn how it differs.) However, the concept of making the most money with your strong hands and losing the least money with your weaker hands is the same in both types of poker.

Think of your stack of chips as your army. The more chips you have, the greater your strength and ability to attack the enemy. The smaller your chip count, the fewer soldiers you have to fight the enemy, making you more vulnerable.

Your goal is to preserve and add to your stack of chips, build your army, in both tournaments and cash games. The main difference between the two is that you can always add more chips to your stack between hands in a cash game, but you cannot reach into your pocket for more money during a tournament.

Playing solid poker in no-limit hold'em is the best approach to both tournaments and cash games. A wild, reckless style of play can help you get hold of a lot of chips, but keeping them is another story. Unless you tighten up your play at some point, you will eventually crash and burn.

10. SOMETIMES GIVE YOUR OPPONENTS MORE RESPECT THAN THEY DESERVE

Unless you have played with your opponents before, assume that they all know what they are doing. If this proves to be false, you can capitalize on your opponents' lack of skill later in the game. Until I see a player making what I consider to be a very bad play, I pretend that they are all great players.

You must get to know the various styles of play that your opponents use, paying special attention to the starting hands they play. Some players obviously deserve more respect than others when they enter a pot, and it is your job to be aware of who these players are and act accordingly.

I also believe that being polite and respectful to your opponents is necessary. I don't like to see people get angry or upset with each other at the table because it often causes unnecessary tension and even forces some of your opponents to quit the game.

Poker is a fun game, and it is even more fun when people are laughing and having a good time. If your opponents are enjoying themselves, they are less likely to become upset when they lose their money, and will continue playing as long as they are having a good time. Respect others as both people and players.

10 Practice Hands

In this section you will learn how to play certain types of no-limit hold'em hands according to your position in the betting sequence. Whether you are sitting in an early, middle or late position is especially important in no-limit hold'em because you risk your entire stack of chips every time you play a hand, whereas in limit hold'em, you risk only one or more bets that are limited in size.

The number of players who have the advantage of getting to act after you have acted becomes all the more important, especially when you are sitting one or two seats to the left of the big blind.

Because your position in the betting sequence is so important in no-limit Texas hold'em, we have divided each Practice Hand into three parts: Early Position, Middle Position, and Late Position. When we mention the word raise in this section, we mean that you increase the bet by 3-4 times the size of the big blind.

Now, let's review these Practice Hands, complete with card illustrations!

Practice Hand # 1
Two Aces

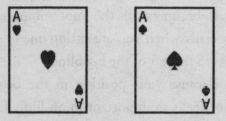

What is the best hand that you can start with in no-limit hold'em? Aces, of course. But there's an old saying in poker that aces win small pots and lose big pots. I disagree with this old adage, because I believe that if you play aces the right way in all situations, you can win with them more often than you lose. Let's start with how to play A-A from a front position.

Early Position

People have different ideas on how to play pocket aces from an early table position. Some players like to raise while others prefer just calling. Raising will help you force some of your opponents to fold, meaning that you will have fewer people to beat in order to win the pot. But you take the risk of winning less money when fewer players are in the pot.

Just calling the size of the big blind (limping) can deceive your opponents into entering the pot because they think that you have a mediocre hand, so the pot probably will be bigger than it would have been if you had raised. But you take the risk of having to play against more opponents, any one of whom could beat your aces if they have a drawing hand or a lower pair and hit the flop just right.

I don't like my odds of winning with my pocket aces when I have three or more opponents because I know that pocket pairs stand a better chance against only one or two opponents. Therefore I recommend raising three to four times the size of the big blind when you have pocket aces in an early position.

Middle Position

If the pot has been opened or raised by a player sitting in one of the first three seats to the left of the big blind, you can either reraise or just call. It depends on the kind of game you're playing in.

Suppose you're in an action game. A player comes in for the minimum bet, you also just call, two or three other players limp in after you, and then a guy who raises almost every pot puts in a raise.

In other words, there are four or five limpers before anybody raises the pot. Good! By just calling, you have set up the raiser so that you can reraise.

If you reraise right there, your opponents might figure that you are just trying to steal the pot, or that you have an A-K, but they hardly ever put you on aces because you just called the first time you had a chance to bet. If you're in any other type of game, raise with aces and reraise if a raise is already in the pot.

Late Position

Always raise or reraise with aces from a late position. After everyone has passed to the button, you sometimes will see people limp with pocket aces. That's not a good idea! The chances that a player will raise from either of the two blinds are slim since you have two of the four aces in the deck locked up.

If neither of the blinds raise, they're going to get free cards on the flop with any kind of oddball hand. And then you will have no idea of where you are with your aces when the flop comes with 8-4-3, for example, and one of the blinds bets into you. That's why you should raise with aces when you're in late position.

It doesn't matter how many people are already in the pot, raise. If someone has raised in front of you with a lot of players in the pot, reraise.

You cannot give free cards very often (especially in a tournament) if you want to win. A lot of times, too, your opponents will discount the strength of your hand when you make a late-position raise and they will play with you because they believe that you're just trying to steal the pot.

Any time that you have pocket aces, you want someone to come after you with a raise. Then your decision is whether to just flat-call and try to nail him after the flop, or move in immediately to try to win the pot right there.

If you flat-call, there's always the danger that your opponent will out-flop you, however that's just a part of the game. When you're playing aces in no-limit poker, you're always trying to maximize the amount of money that you can win with your hand, so you choose the strategy that will best serve that purpose.

The Blinds

It's great to be dealt pocket aces, but the worst place you can get them is in the small blind or the big blind. Why? Because you're in the weakest table position of all at the start of the hand. After the flop, you will always have to act first.

Therefore, when you have pocket aces in one of the blinds, it is more important to raise than it is from any other position to try to get as many other players to fold their hands as possible. Most reasonable players will pay attention when one of the blinds raises, because they know that he must have a very strong hand.

Now suppose everybody checks to the button. He raises and the small blind folds. You're sitting in the big blind with pocket aces. How do you play them in this situation?

You might try to trap him by just flat-calling the raise in the hope that something will come on the flop that hits him a little bit but hits you even better. For example, he might have raised with a hand such as A-6 and think that he has the best hand if either an ace or a six hits the flop.

To summarize, pocket aces is such a powerful hand that you raise with them most of the time from any position, no matter what other players do in front of you or behind you. And then you pray that lady luck will deal just the right flop!

Practice Hand # 2
Two Kings

You've been dealt two kings, the second-best starting hand in no-limit Texas hold'em. You're ready to shout for joy—but wait! Pocket kings can be one of the most dangerous hands in poker. Why? Because it is so hard to fold before the flop if an opponent puts in a big raise. And if somebody with an ace in his hand calls when you raise before the flop, you're a goner if an ace comes on the flop.

So, how do you play pocket kings? Usually, if an opponent raises in front of you, reraise with your two kings. Of course, there's always the chance that you will run into two aces, or a "big" ace, or even "any ace," but that's a chance you'll just have to take in a cash game. But in a tournament, any time the flop is raised and reraised before it gets to you, you're probably better off folding your two kings. Even if you are wrong once in a while, you'll save a lot of money in the long run.

Early Position

Suppose you're playing in a $50 buy-in no-limit hold'em tournament and you are in the middle stage of the event. You are Player A, the first to act, and you have been dealt pocket kings. How do you play the hand before the flop?

You can raise three or four times the size of the big blind, or you can just call with the two kings from a front position in the hope that someone will raise.

The reason that you might just call with the kings is to let somebody raise behind you so that you can reraise and win the pot right there. If somebody behind you has pocket aces and raises the pot, there's nothing you can do about it.

You're caught between a rock and a hard place, so you just call the reraise and wait to see if a handsome cowboy comes out of hiding on the flop. If a player just calls your raise, you still have the second-best hand that you can start with. Just hope that no ace comes on the board.

Say that you limp with the kings, Player B raises, and Player C calls the raise. What should you do? Reraise.

More than likely, you will win the pot right there, unless either Player B or C has aces or queens. If either one of them reraises you, you're in trouble. If Player B has aces, for example, he will move you all-in, but if he doesn't do that, there's a pretty good chance that you have the best hand.

Middle Position

Play pocket kings from a middle position similar to how you would play aces. Your main goal is to eliminate other players, especially the people who are in a later position that you. You want to play your pocket kings head-up against just one opponent.

If there are lots of action players in the game who haven't acted yet, you can just call with the intention of reraising. But if the people who get to act after you are tight players, definitely raise three to four times the size of the big blind if you are the first one in the pot.

If a player has raised in front of you, almost always reraise. If you reraise and an opponent moves all in against your reraise, you will have a big decision to make. Does he have pocket aces or could he have a lesser pair?

In no-limit hold'em, when an opponent puts all his chips into the pot after two players have already raised in front of him, you can be sure that he has a big hand. How big is the question you have to answer.

Late Position

Play pocket kings from a late table position almost the same way you would play aces. Never limp into the pot with them. You want any player who has a big ace to fold. You also want anyone who has a smaller pair or a small ace to fold. When I refer to a player with a big ace or one with a small ace, I am referring to the rank of his kicker. An A-Q, for example, is a big ace. An A-4 is a small ace.

Pocket kings is a more vulnerable hand than pocket aces, of course. When you have kings, there are four aces in the deck that could beat you on the flop. And that is why you need to protect your kings as much as you can by raising or reraising before the flop.

Practice Hand # 3
Two Queens

Two queens is sometimes a very difficult hand to play in no-limit hold'em. It's almost always too good to fold but it's also very vulnerable against A-K, as well as K-K and A-A. Often, your success in a tournament depends on the times when you push with queens and the times when you fold them.

If you're not mentally prepared to fold two queens when you need to, you'd better not be playing no-limit hold'em. There are a lot of scenarios where pocket queens is a great hand, but there also are a lot of situations where it isn't.

Early Position

Do not **slow-play** (just call) with queens from an early position because any ace or king that comes on the flop will put you in jeopardy. You want to bring them in for a raise in order to get some money into the pot. But if a player reraises a substantial portion of his chips before the flop, pocket queens is not the type of hand that you want to take a stand with. You should release them in this scenario. Making laydowns when it is correct to do so is just as important as making the right calls and raises.

Suppose you have pocket queens against one opponent and the flop comes J-8-2. You make a bet and he calls. You can beat hands such as A-J, Q-J, and 10-9. Ask yourself, "What cards could my opponent have?" He may have pocket eights or a straight draw. Or he may have slow-played (just called before the flop) with aces or kings.

Suppose a four comes on the turn. Should you check or bet? Queens is not a hand that you can afford to give a free card with. Go ahead and bet again. If you check, you face the possibility that an ace or king will come on the river and you will lose a hand that you should have won.

Generally speaking, never give a free card when you think you have the best hand, especially in tournaments.

Middle Position

Pocket queens is not a big enough hand to just call with. Your main goal is to eliminate players and try to win the hand either before the flop or on the flop. Therefore you need to make a big enough raise so that it will be unprofitable for the opposition to call and get a chance to draw out against you.

If one or two people have already limped into the pot, make your raise more than three or four times the size of the big blind. For example, suppose the blinds are $25-$50 and two people in front of you have just called for $50. It's your turn to act, so make it around $300 to go. If someone has raised in front you—for example, they have made it $200 to go—make it about $600 to go.

If you get called and neither an ace nor a king comes on the flop, you can make a pot-sized bet and try to win the hand right there. If you get called, you will need to decide what type of hand your opponent has and act accordingly on the next round of betting. As you can see, pocket queens can be a tough hand to play at times.

Late Position

If you hold queens in late position or on the button and a few players have limped in front of you, your queens increase in value. The chances are that no players behind you (the blinds) have bigger pairs than yours. In this situation, always raise with pocket queens. Then if the flop comes with small cards, you can try to win the pot right there.

Your biggest decision when you have pocket queens is not how to play them when you have the best hand, but whether you can fold them when you have the worst hand.

Pocket queens is the third-best starting hand in hold'em and should be recognized as such, but always remember that as the rank of your pair gets smaller, there are more and more higher pairs and overcards that can beat your hand.

Practice Hand # 4
Jacks and Tens

Jacks and tens are two of the most difficult hands to play in no-limit hold'em. Although you'd rather have pocket jacks than tens, one advantage of tens is that a ten can make a straight, and it is less likely that someone else can make a straight because you have two of them in your hand.

Just remember that if you don't flop a set when you have pocket tens, there are four bigger cards that can beat you. So if an overcard hits the flop, you can't play your hand with any confidence. With tens, you are a "favorite" to see one or more overcards on the flop, whereas with jacks, it's about even money.

If you are the first one in the pot, you can bring it in for a raise. If you are reraised, do not hesitate to throw your tens away.

Now suppose there is a limper in early position and you are in second position. Should you raise with pocket tens? I am very leery of raising in this spot because if I get raised by a player sitting behind me, I probably don't have the best hand.

However, if there is a limper in early position and you're sitting in one of the last two seats, you definitely can raise with pocket tens. If the limper comes **back over the top** (reraises), you can fold.

Suppose that you have pocket jacks or tens one spot in front of the button (the cutoff seat). You raise and the big blind calls.

The board comes:

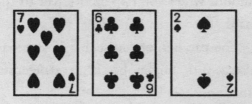

The big blind checks to you and you bet. Then the big blind reraises. What do you do? You can't possibly like your hand when someone raises you. Your opponent either thinks you're on a steal, or he has a big hand and is trying to suck you in. If you have only a relatively small amount of chips left in a tournament, you might call, but if you have a lot of chips, you probably should pass.

There are situations when your opponent might raise with a pair of nines or eights or an A-7, for example. If you know how he plays, you should be able to decide whether to continue with the hand or simply fold. In other words, be very cautious when you flop an overpair to the board.

You can bet, of course, but if someone raises, you might be in a dangerous situation.

Early to Middle Position

From early to middle position, you can raise with pocket jacks or tens, especially if you're the first one in the pot. Just decide in advance that you aren't going to call a raise. If someone raises behind you, it's usually time to bail out. You also can limp with pocket jacks or tens from early to middle position. If anyone raises before the flop, usually pass.

For example, in the early stages of a big buy-in tournament when lots of chips are in play, just calling a minimum bet certainly is a viable strategy. On the flop, you want to hit a set and if you don't, you can get away from them without losing much money because you only limped before the flop.

Late Position

Suppose you are in late position, five or six players have passed, and then one player enters the pot for the minimum bet. In this scenario, you should bring it in for a raise with pocket jacks or tens.

How you play jacks or tens in a tournament is always a question of using the best tournament strategy. There are times in tournaments when you might play tens like you would play deuces— especially in the early stages of a big buy-in tournament when lots of chips are in play and the blinds are small.

Other times, in the later stages of the tournament, you might have to go all in with your tens because of your chip position. If you aren't willing to modify your style of play according to the situation, you can get broke to jacks or tens very easily.

Practice Hand # 5
Middle and Small Pairs

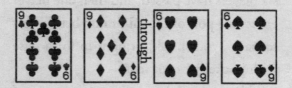

Middle Pairs

The bigger the pocket pair the better off you are, and the smaller the pair the more vulnerable you are. However, there isn't a lot of difference in how you play any of the middle pairs. Nines are a little stronger than eights or sevens and you play them similar to the way that you play tens. Just remember that you don't have the straight possibility with nines that you have with tens.

You cannot stand much pressure from other players when you have a middle pair and you don't want to play too aggressively with any middle pair.

Middle pairs should be played cautiously. You can raise with them from late position if you are the first one in the pot, but be prepared to pitch them if you get played with. If you get called, play them very cautiously after the flop.

In tournaments, your chip position often dictates how you play middle pairs. There are times when you are forced to play them—for example when you are very low on chips and believe that you probably won't get a better hand to play. This is about the only time when you take a stand with the middle pairs and go all in.

Small Pairs

Suppose you have made it to the final table in a no-limit hold'em tournament.

The table is six-handed and you look down at pocket sixes on the button. The action is passed to you. What do you do?

In this situation, it might be okay to make a small raise with your low pair. For example, say that the antes are $200 and the blinds are $400-$800 at a six-handed table. There is $2,400 in the pot. You have $15,000 in front of you. If you want to raise, why not bring it in for $3,000?

If you get reraised, you can fold the hand before the flop. And if you get out-flopped, you can fold it on the flop. But what are you going to do if you move in your whole stack and get called? This is why you should play small pairs even more cautiously than you play medium pairs.

If you have two sixes, for example, and your opponent has an 8-7, the 8-7 is only a slight underdog to your pair of sixes. In fact, any two overcards are only a small underdog to a pair. And if the overcards are suited, they are a slightly smaller dog to the pair. This is why you should not play very aggressively with a low pocket pair.

Practice Hand # 6 Ace-King

To win a no-limit hold'em tournament, you have to win when you have A-K and you have to beat A-K when an opponent has it. Although it may not be the final hand, A-K often will be the deciding hand, the one with which you win or lose the most chips. Big Slick is the biggest "decision" hand in tournament play.

Ace-king is a drawing hand, not a made hand. You will flop a pair to A-K about 30 percent of the time. If you go to the river with it, you will make a pair about 50 percent of the time. I believe that A-K is the most frequently misplayed hand in no-limit hold'em.

Players call with it in situations where a raise would be the better play. They move in with A-K when they probably should fold. And they often misplay A-K after the flop. Big Slick can be a very profitable hand, but it also can send you to the rail.

Early Position

When I am sitting in an early position, I like to make a standard raise of three to four times the size of the big blind if I am the first player to enter the pot. If I'm playing in the early stage of a tournament and an opponent makes a big reraise before the flop, I usually will fold.

If only one player has entered the pot before it is my turn to act, I will raise if I suspect that my opponent is weak. But if I suspect that he has a big hand and is just trying to trap me, I will just flat-call his bet. Knowing how your opponents play will help you in making decisions like this.

Middle Position

When you are sitting in a middle position at the table, raise the standard amount if you are the first player in the pot—don't ever just flat-call from middle position if you are the first player in the pot.

A-K is not a hand that you should slow-play in this situation because it is a drawing hand, not a made hand. But if two or more people have limped into the pot for the minimum bet, be inclined to just call, especially if you're playing in the early stage of a tournament.

What if only one person has limped into the pot? You can either raise or you can just flat-call depending on what kind of hand strength you think your opponent has.

If the pot has been raised before it gets to me, I usually will just call and see the flop. If the flop gives my A-K no help whatsoever, I will fold if someone bets.

Late Position

The betting action that has happened before it is my turn to act is the determining factor in how I play A-K when I am sitting in a late position at the table.

If one player has raised from an early position and two players have called the raise, I usually will also call. I want to see what develops on the flop. But if someone has moved in all his chips before it's my turn to act, I will fold.

What if no one has entered the pot and I am on or next to the button? In that case, I will raise. And if only one or two of my opponents have entered the pot for the minimum bet, I will raise if I think they are weak players. It's a lot easier to decide what to do with Big Slick when you're in late position, isn't it? Ditto for a lot of other hands.

The Blinds

Seldom raise from either of the blinds if two or more limpers already are in the pot. You don't have good position after the flop – in fact, you have the worst position at the table – and if you get reraised, you could be in a ton of trouble.

One of the advantages of not raising with A-K is that you often will get action from lesser hands if you flop top pair. Players are accustomed to seeing opponents raise with A-K, so they probably won't give you credit for having such a strong hand since you didn't raise with it before the flop.

Should you ever raise with A-K from one of the blinds? Yes, when you are the small blind and nobody has entered pot, meaning that you will be playing the hand head-up against the big blind. In that case, raise the standard amount. Another time when you might raise is when you are the big blind and the small blind has called for half a bet. If you think he has a weak hand, make a standard raise.

Practice Hand # 7
Ace-Queen, Ace-Jack and Ace-Ten

Ace-Queen

Ace-queen is a trouble hand that you should play cautiously. You don't want to put a lot of money in the pot with A-Q (suited or unsuited) from an early position.

Treat being suited as a bonus, something that should not change how you play the hand. Although I prefer suited cards when I play an A-Q, A-J or A-10, I value their ranks more than their suitedness.

You cannot call a reraise before the flop with A-Q in the opening rounds of a tournament. If you are sitting in middle to late position and there are other limpers in the pot, you can call with A-Q in order to see the flop cheaply.

If nobody has entered the pot, raise a modest amount of about three to four times the size of the big blind. If anyone reraises, fold. If you flop top pair, usually make a pot-sized bet on the flop. Later in the tournament, particularly when you're playing at a shorthanded table, A-Q goes up in value. When you're either short stacked or are up against a short stack, you might even go all in with the hand.

Ace-Jack or Ace-Ten

A-J and A-10 are even more troublesome to play than A-Q. You can't afford to call any raises with these hands before the flop. A-J is a little bit stronger than A-10 because of its higher kicker. A-10 gains some value from the 10—although it is a weak kicker, the 10 can make a straight. Being suited is strictly a bonus.

Generally speaking, these are calling hands from middle to late position when others have entered the pot for the minimum bet. You sometimes can raise with them from late position when no one has entered, but discard them if anyone reraises.

You would like to flop a straight or a straight draw, or a jack (or ten) because then you have the best kicker (the Ace).

Practice Hand # 8
Ace-Wheel Card

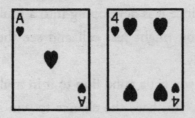

An ace with a small card, suited or unsuited, is not a hand that you should play from an early position. It is of little value to you from a front position. Why? Because if an ace comes on the flop and you bet—and an opponent calls or raises—you have a bad kicker and are in danger of losing to an ace with a high kicker. Obviously, the best flop for ace-small suited is three to your suit or three wheel cards. But the odds are so great against getting that kind of flop that if you play ace-small every time you are dealt it, you will be a big loser.

Now suppose you are in middle to late position and a couple of limpers are in the pot. Since it is developing into a multiway pot, you might just call and see the flop cheaply.

If you get a good flop to it in multiway action, you have the chance to win a nice pot. You don't want to call a raise with A-4 and you don't want to play it heads up. Therefore when you call for the minimum bet, be prepared to throw your hand away if someone raises.

Suppose you're on the button and no one has entered the pot. Should you raise with ace-small? No. Suppose the small blind calls the raise. What could he have?

He probably has an ace in his hand or a pocket pair. And almost any kicker that he has with his ace will be higher than your wheel card. Even if his kicker is a wheel card as well, you still are not a favorite to the hand most of the time if an ace falls on the flop.

When you are in the small blind against the big blind only, you have three options: raise, fold or call.

If you just call, you might get yourself into trouble. If you fold, you stay out of trouble. If you raise, you might win the pot right there. It depends on how you feel about it.

For example, if you have observed that your opponent usually defends his blind, usually just complete the bet against this type of opponent.

If he is someone who raises all the time, he might raise just because you limped. What you decide to do depends on the type of player your opponent is.

What about playing hands like A-6, A-7, or A-8? None of these ace-middle-card hands can make a straight. Your best result is the nut flush if the hand is suited, or two pair if you hit your kicker. You're just throwing your money away if you play them.

Practice Hand # 9
King-Queen

In no-limit hold'em, K-Q is a trap hand. Unless you flop something like J-10-9, A-J-10, two kings and a queen, or even two pair, you will be in bad shape with this hand. King-queen is a hand that you don't want to play in a nine-handed ring game, in particular, from an early or a middle position.

I give a little more value to J-10 because you can make more straights with the hand than you can make with either K-Q or Q-J.

Early to Middle Position

Fold!

Late Position

Suppose you're playing in a tournament and are dealt K-Q. The action is passed to you on the button. How do you play the hand? You might raise to try to knock out the two blinds, but that is the only circumstance in which you should consider raising with it.

Although K-Q suited is better than K-Q offsuit, being suited doesn't increase its value very much. It is still the type of hand that can get you into big trouble.

Now suppose you are on the button with K-Q and a player raises in front of you. What do you do? You can get into trouble if you call the raise. Fold.

K-Q in the Blinds

Suppose you are in the little blind with a K-Q. Everybody else has passed. Now what do you do? In this case, you can raise the big blind, even though you are out of position and will have to act first after the flop. Some players will call a small raise from the big blind with hands that aren't very good because they already have money in the pot, but the chances are good that you'll win the pot right there with your pre-flop raise.

Practice Hand # 10
Middle Suited Connectors

Middle connectors are hands that you play in cash games to try to win a big pot in multiway action. But in tournaments, you face a big problem with these types of hands: You can't put more money on the table when you lose all your chips like you can in cash games. When you lose your stack, you're out of action. And that is why you seldom play middle connectors in tournaments.

Early Position

You simply do not play hands such as 9-8 suited or offsuit, 8-7 or 7-6 from an early position in no-limit hold'em because you cannot call a raise with them.

Furthermore, you will be in a bad betting position from the flop onward. Always remember that the chips you do not lose on mediocre hands in bad position will be available to you later to possibly double or triple up with on your good hands.

Late Position

When two or more players have entered the pot for the minimum bet, you can occasionally play middle connectors from the cutoff seat or the button. But suppose everyone passes to you on the button and you have the 9♠ 8♠. What do you do? Fold.

Remember that if nobody in front of you has a hand, somebody behind you might have one. I call it the **bunching factor**, meaning that if no one has big cards in front of you, it is somewhat more likely that big cards are **bunched** behind you.

The only other time that it might be okay to play hands such as 9-8 in no-limit hold'em is when you hold them in the big blind in an unraised pot.

You also can call for one-half a bet from the small blind. However if the big blind raises, throw the hand away. Remember that a lot of people play ace-anything—A-10, A-9, A-8—for the minimum bet so that if you hit a nine or eight on the flop, the chances are good that someone will have a better kicker. Just because any two cards can win in hold'em doesn't mean that you should play them.

Shane's Review Questions

1. Why is your position in the betting sequence so important in no-limit hold'em?

Because if you are the first bettor and someone raises behind you, you can lose all your chips if you are wrong about the strength of your hand. However, if you don't have to act until most of your opponents have acted, you can better judge how strong your hand is and how much money you should bet or raise.

2. If you are dealt pocket jacks, how likely is it that an ace, king or queen will flop?

It's about even money that an overcard to your jacks will come on the flop. That is why pockets jacks are so tricky to play correctly. They look like such a big pair—until an overcard comes on the flop!

3. Why should you play only big pairs and A-K when you are in early position?

You are at a disadvantage by being one of the first players who must act in all the betting rounds, so you need the advantage of having high cards to compensate for your poor position in the betting sequence.

4. If you are sitting one seat in front of the button with pocket kings and only one player has entered the pot for the minimum amount, what should you do?

Raise four or five times the size of the big blind. You want to play heads-up against the first bettor or win the pot by raising before the flop. Do not just call because the button and the two blinds, who get to act after you do, might also just call and catch a lucky flop to beat you.

5. Why is it important to know whether the big blind is a loose player or a tight player?

If you know that the big blind is a loose player who likes to play a lot of hands, you should only raise with premium hands when he is in the big blind because he won't fold very often.

But if the big blind is a tight player who only plays premium hands, you can raise with a marginal hand when he is in the big blind. You should do this because he usually will fold anything except good cards, thus giving you a better chance of stealing his blind bet.

6. If you are in middle position with an A-Q and nobody has entered the pot, what should you do?

An A-Q is the type of hand that you should raise with when you are sitting in a middle or late position and everybody else has folded in front of you. No-limit hold'em is a bettor's game, not a caller's game. Therefore if your cards are good enough to play, raise if you are the first player to enter the pot.

7. Suppose two players have limped into the pot for the minimum bet. You have pocket aces on the button and raise six times the size of the big blind to try to drive them out of the pot so that you can win it right there.

But alas, they both call your big raise! The flop comes with the 8♦ 7♦ 6♦. One opponent makes a big bet and another player calls. What should you do?

Uh oh! Even though you started with the best possible hand in hold'em, it's time to bail out of your sinking ship to save some money. You're beaten. Fold.

How Would You Play This Hand?

PLAYING POCKET KINGS IN A BIG TOURNAMENT

Jack was still feeling the agony of defeat from getting drawn out on when he had the best hand in the $2,000 buy-in no-limit hold'em tournament at the World Series of Poker. He emailed me his pitiful story. "I was on the button with pocket kings," he began. "Everybody else folded. I had about $8,000 in chips, and the blinds were $200-$400."

How Would You Play This Hand Before the Flop?

    a. Fold

    b. Call the size of the big blind

    c. Raise

Here's How Jack Played It

"I made a small raise of $400, trying not to scare off the blinds. The small blind folded and the big blind, who had about $9,000 in chips, raised $1,600. I reraised all the rest of my chips ($8,000) and he called.

I thought that he probably had an ace, but judging from his actions and his strong raise, I didn't think he had pocket aces. I was right – he showed me the Q♣ J♣.

"A club came on the flop, another one appeared on the turn, and a third club came on the river to give him a flush and give me a trip to the rail.

I figure that he had only a four percent chance of beating me after the flop. Did I make the correct decision, or should I have played this hand differently?"

Tom's Analysis of Jack's Play

You might have made a slightly bigger starting raise with the pocket kings; for example, $1,200 to go in this situation as opposed to $800. I like to bring it in for a standard raise of between three and four times the amount of the big blind.

You would like to get a little action on your kings. When your opponent plays back at you, the only hand that can beat you before the flop, of course, is pocket aces.

I am fairly fatalistic about this sort of thing. When I run into pocket aces against my pocket kings before the flop, and I have played them strongly, I usually am just going to have to go broke to them.

So, I would have **played back** (reraised) before the flop in just about every situation that I can think of to try to win the pot right there. You simply ran into every tournament poker player's nightmare, a bona-fide bad beat.

If your opponent had made the proper play and folded his hand, he wouldn't even have seen the flop, but obviously, he was willing to gamble.

His reraise wasn't so bad against a rather timid $800 bet by the button. He might have thought that he could steal it from you if you didn't have much of a hand.

But when you played back for all of your chips, it should have been clear to the big blind that he should fold, because the risk of losing with a Q-J was so great.

He should have known that there was virtually no hand that you could have that he would be the favorite against.

Furthermore, he should've realized that if he lost the hand, he would be crippled, going from $9,000 to $1,000 in chips, putting him in bad shape. But your opponent wasn't thinking logically and foisted a genuine bad beat upon you.

An Added Note

The reader who took this beat said that he was surprised to see that the players at the World Series of Poker were typical of what he finds in the less important, smaller buy-in tournaments that he plays. "I saw some great players, some bad players, but mostly average players. I was really expecting *all* players to be great players," he said.

Although you are going to find the world's greatest players participating in many of the events at the WSOP, it is a misconception that all the players are world-class. The tremendous diversity in the playing styles and skills that you find at the Series is due in large part to the satellite system.

Players who are average, inexperienced, loose, tight, world-class, reckless, amateurs, or pros—anyone can win a satellite. And most WSOP entrants these days get into the main event through a satellite win.

You'll see the entire gamut of player expertise at the World Series, but what sets it apart from the other tournaments is that, competing at virtually every table, you will find players who have distinguished themselves in the fields of battle—players who have won WSOP bracelets or have had high money finishes or have won other major tournaments.

Poker is unique in that amateur players are actively encouraged to compete against pros, whereas this certainly is not true of other sports. The only requirement for playing a poker tournament, of course, is that you post the buy-in. And in today's satellite-oriented tournament system, you don't even have to pay full price for your seat—you can win it at a bargain price via a satellite.

PLAYING BIG SLICK IN A $60 NO-LIMIT HOLD'EM TOURNAMENT

How much should you bet or raise in no-limit hold'em tournaments? Probably more novice players have asked me this question than any other.

I suggest that you usually raise three or four times the size of the big blind. I recommend this standard raise instead of varying the size of your bets—betting more with a strong hand and less with a weaker one—so that your opponents cannot guess the strength of your hand based on the size of your bet. David, an E-correspondent, ran into a problem with bet size in a tournament that he recently played. "I was playing in a no-limit hold'em tournament with a $60 buy-in and one optional $25 rebuy," he began. "I doubled my initial stack of $500 in chips to $1,000 in chips during the first 40 minutes of play. I was sitting in a middle position when I looked down at the A♣ K♣. Nobody had entered the pot yet."

How Would You Play This Hand Before the Flop?

    a. Pass

    b. Raise a large amount

    c. Raise a small amount

Here's How David Played It

"I bet one-half my stack. A gentleman sitting two seats to my left with a bigger stack than mine went all in. Everyone else folded. I studied him for a moment before I acted."

How Would You Play This Hand Against a Raise?

    a. Fold

    b. Call the raise

    c. Reraise

Here's How David Played It

"I called the raise for several reasons. His manner suggested to me that he wasn't completely confident with his all-in move. I put him on a pair of kings or queens and figured that even if he had kings, I could catch an ace to beat him, plus I also had straight and flush potential with my suited A-K.

If I won I would double my stack again and put myself in a commanding lead in the tournament. And if I lost, I still could rebuy.

Needless to say, his pocket kings held up (otherwise I wouldn't be writing you!) and I have been rethinking my decision ever since. What's your opinion of my play?"

Tom's Analysis of David's Play

You made a mistake, David, by betting half of your stack on your initial raise. Although you don't say in your E-letter, I assume that the blinds were around $25-$50 at that point in the tournament, in which case the standard bet would have been $150 to $200.

Calling the raiser's bet with the remainder of your chips was marginal, although I somewhat can justify it because one-half of your chips already were in the pot. However, if you were positive that your opponent had aces or kings—which indeed he did—you should have folded.

You overbet the pot to start with and that is what created this bad situation in which you put yourself. If you had made a standard raise of three or four times the big blind, you could have gotten away from your hand much more easily when your opponent made his all-in bet.

Online Hold'em:
The Pajama Game

The Basics of
Online Poker

As simple as it sounds, the first thing you need to do to play online Internet poker is to own or have access to a computer. Then you need to know some basics of how to operate a computer, such as how to turn it on or off, how to use a mouse, how to obtain access to the Internet, and so on.

Any 10-year-old child probably knows more about how to operate a computer than I did when I first began playing online, so don't feel dumb if you don't know the basic skills yet. Once you learn a few simple things, then you will find out how easy it is to work with a computer and you can go to the next step, getting on the Internet.

There are literally dozens of online poker rooms, with more cropping up all the time. Your first order of business is to decide which site or sites you want to play on. Currently the biggest site as far as number of games is PartyPoker.com. PokerStars.com is the second largest site followed by UltimateBet.com and ParadisePoker.com.

In addition to the big four, you will find numerous other sites that have an attractive array of online games for all size bankrolls. New Internet poker rooms continue to open as online poker becomes more and more popular. New sites almost always offer sign-up bonuses to players, such as adding $40 to your account when you deposit $100 to start.

Once you have chosen a poker room you like, the next order of business is to download that site's software onto your computer. How do you do that?

First you access Internet Explorer or one of the search engines and type in www.pokerstars.com, for example, and the computer will take you to the site. On the front page of the web site, you will find instructions about how to download the software, such as "click here to install."

If you are not successful the first time you try, don't give up—simply go back and start over again. Ask for help from a friend if necessary, or contact a representative of the virtual poker room to guide you through the process. The web site will usually tell you how to contact one of its employees if you need assistance.

After you have successfully downloaded the software, a small symbol (an icon), will appear on your computer screen. Whenever you want to play, you simply double click the icon with your mouse and it will take you to the site. The icon usually has the name of the site on it, so it is easy to find.

Setting Up An Account

Now that you have downloaded the software and your handy icon has been planted on your computer screen for future use, what comes next? You must set up an account with that site so that you can start playing.

To set up an account, double click on the site's icon and when the site appears on your screen, double click the "Set Up an Account" button. It will ask you to fill in some basic information, such as your name, mailing address, and e-mail address. It also will ask you to choose a **handle**.

214

What is a handle? It's simply the name you choose to play under. Your handle can be any name you want within a certain number of letters. You can use something like "Poker Bill" or "Lucky Dana" or even your real name.

If the handle you have chosen is already taken, you must choose a different name, or simply put a number after the name you prefer such as Lucky Dana 7. You also must choose a password that only you know, such as the name of your pet dog or cat, or a favorite relative with a number or two thrown in that you can easily remember. People often use a favorite food such as lobster or cookies as part of their password, or even just a series of numbers such as someone's birthday.

The purpose of the password is to protect you so that nobody but you can have access to your account. Online poker rooms usually suggest that you change your password for your own protection about every six months.

Once you have set up an account, the site will e-mail a verification letter to you. Once you have responded to the e-mail, your account is active and you are finally eligible to play poker.

Playing with Funny Money

What, we get to play for free now? Well, yes and no. Practically every site allows you a certain amount of play money so that you can test the software, get used to handling the mouse properly, learn how to bet, fold and raise, and so on for free.

No real money changes hands, you're playing to have fun and get some practice. But sooner or later, mostly sooner, you are going to want to play for real money.

Funding Your Account

Online poker rooms offer several different ways to fund your account. Some sites still allow the use of credit cards while others do not. Some sites allow you to send them a check and when it clears, your account is credited for the amount of the check. Most sites allow the use of Neteller, which is what I use.

Neteller is a company that allows you to put money into a Neteller account directly from your checking or savings account. Once money is in your Neteller account you can make deposits directly into your online poker account.

If you want to withdraw money from your online poker account, you reverse the process by re-depositing the money into your Neteller account, and then notifying Neteller when you want the money transferred back into your bank account. Transactions often take four or five business days.

There are other ways to accomplish the same thing faster, but I have found that Neteller is safe. Each site will give you various options on how you can fund your poker account; decide what method suits you best.

Now Let's Play Poker Online

Finally, you're going to play some poker—from the comfort of your home, in your pajamas if you prefer. I know one player who has a remote keyboard and plays poker online while he's trudging away on his home treadmill. Another has her computer set up on the patio and sun bathes while she plays poker. Don't try playing online while you're in the shower, but just about any other setting will work.

Most sites offer games and limits for every bankroll. Some virtual poker rooms have games with limits as low as 2¢-4¢ with no rake. From there, the limits can go all the way up to $100-$200 and sometimes even higher. Pot-limit and no-limit games, usually hold'em or Omaha, also are available.

When you first start playing online, choose a game at limits that are comfortable for you, whether $1-$2 seven-card stud, $10-$20 Omaha high-low, or 2¢-4¢ Texas hold'em. But before your first card is dealt, be sure to study the Top 10 Tips I have prepared for new online poker players.

Now that you're ready to start playing online for real money, here are my top ten tips on how to win at Internet poker. If you follow my suggestions, you have an excellent chance of not only having a lot of fun, but also winning some extra cash. Personally, the more money I win, the more fun I have!

Tom's Top 10 Winning Tips

1. CONCENTRATE ON STRONG STARTING HANDS AND YOUR POSITION AT THE TABLE

The saying goes that Omaha high-low is a low-card game, seven-card stud is a live-card game, and Texas hold'em is a high-card game. But Texas hold'em is more than simply a high-card game, it also is a positional game. That is, you must have good cards and good position in the betting sequence to be a winner at hold'em.

Strong starting hands such as aces, kings, queens, and A-K can usually be played from any seating position at the table. You usually raise or reraise with these hands and try to eliminate as many players from the pot as possible. Why do you want to eliminate the competition before the flop?

Because the fewer the players in the pot, the greater the chances that your big pair or A-K can win without improvement. The more players in the pot, the greater the possibility that someone will flop something, even if its only a draw, that will beat you.

With lots of players drawing at you, even if you have the best hand on the flop, you are in grave danger of getting beaten by the end of the hand.

What do we do about position? Last action is always preferred. The later you have to act in the betting sequence, the more advantage you have in each individual hand. Getting to act after everybody else gives you a chance to see what all the other players are doing before the action gets around to you.

This does not mean you should play extremely weak starting hands just because you have the button. But it does mean that you can play a few more hands than you would if you had to act from an earlier position.

The earlier you have to act after the big blind, the worse your position is. Therefore you need a much stronger hand to enter the pot with when you are sitting in early position than you do in late position.

The reason for this is that you may be subjected to one or more raises by the players who have the advantage of acting after you do.

A hand such as 9-8 suited, which can be played in late position for one bet, is not playable from very early position because it isn't strong enough to call a raise.

When you are sitting in the small or big blind, you have the worst position of all after the flop. Always consider that you will have bad position after the flop in deciding whether your hand is strong enough to **defend your blind** (call a raise) in the event that someone raises before the flop.

For example, suppose you have that marginal 9-8 suited mentioned above. In order to justify calling a raise from either the small or big blind, several other callers must already be in the pot. This is not a hand that you want to play heads-up against a raiser who has better position than you have.

Always keep in mind that when you are in one of the blinds, you will be in the worst betting position from the flop onward—you will not have the advantage of knowing what your opponents have on their minds after the flop. Pearls of wisdom: He who acts last acts with the best information.

2. AVOID PLAYING TOO LOOSE ONLINE

One thing you will soon discover when you're playing low-limit poker online is that most players see too many flops and play too many hands. In other words, they play loose as a goose.

One possible reason is that many low-limit players are new to the game and they want to play a lot of hands—they like action. It's a lot more fun to play than it is to fold and watch others play, right? Just remember that it isn't how many pots you play, it's how much money you win that really counts. As for me, like I said before, the more money I make, the more fun I have.

The way to beat these super loose low-limit games is to play tighter than your opponents are playing. Playing tighter means that you play fewer hands than you may want to play. You also avoid playing weak or marginal hands when you are in an early position, or when the pot has been raised in front of you.

Another way to increase your win in loose low-limit games is to avoid bluffing. In low-limit games you are going to have to show down a hand most of the time, especially in limit hold'em games.

People have a tendency to bluff too often, probably because they have been watching too much "television poker" where they have seen world-class players successfully bluff each other in critical situations. But believe me when I say that bluffing is not the way to play in small online games.

Low-limit players who are new to the game often will excuse an unsuccessful bluffing attempt by saying something like, "I didn't make my flush, so the only way I could win the pot was to bet." Wrong!

The only way to lose an extra bet when you don't make your hand is to bluff-bet, because you're going to get called 98 percent of the time by an opponent, even if he only has a low pair. In low-limit poker games, remember this cardinal rule: Tight is right.

3. PRACTICE READING THE FLOP

If you want to beat Texas hold'em games, you must be able to read the flop. You need to know what the best possible hand is on the flop, the turn and the river.

The best possible hand, called the nuts, can change from card to card. In most hold'em games you won't make the nuts, or run into somebody who has made the nuts, very often. Nevertheless, it is important to know what the best possible hand is at all times.

Since hands are dealt very rapidly online, if you are a new player it might be a good idea to sit out of the game for a few hands (or even an entire round) so that you can practice reading the flop before you begin playing. Pretty soon you should be able to read flops quickly. Like tennis or golf, all it takes is practice.

Reading the flop and getting to know your opponents are absolutely necessary skills in poker. Always ask yourself, "What is the texture of the flop?"

That is, does it contain two or more suited cards or connecting cards that offer flush or straight draws? Is it a high-card flop that has an ace or king? A low-card flop? A

227

rainbow flop with no suited cards? Is this a flop that might have hit one or more of my opponents?

For example, suppose Easy Ed raised before the flop and Dandy Dan called Ed's raise. The flop comes A-Q-4. How likely is it that either Ed or Dan has an ace or queen in their hands?

While you are reading the flop, study your opponents. If you cannot read other players, you can't beat hold'em games. Judging from their betting patterns, try to determine who has a good hand, who is on a draw, and who, if anybody, probably has the nuts or close to it. Trying to determine who has a draw and who has a pair is part of the fun, excitement and strategy of the game.

It is also important to figure out which players have missed the flop completely. What to do with your hand based on

your read of the flop and your opponents
is covered in more detail in other parts of
this book.

4. ADJUST TO THE SPEED OF THE GAME

You will soon discover that online
games are much faster than casino games.
In a typical brick-and-mortar casino
hold'em game, about 30 to 35 hands per
hour are dealt. In online games, around 50
to 55 hands per hour are dealt. The reason
for this is twofold.

First, the cyber dealer deals the cards
must faster than a human dealer. Second,
players cannot deliberate at length when
it is their turn to act. Online poker rooms
have a time clock with a very annoying
beep that reminds players that they must
act on their hands when they have delayed
too long. If the player fails to act on his
hand, his cards are automatically folded.

The good news is that you are able to see more hands per hour online than you can see in a casino. The other good news is that, with practice and experience, you can adjust to this faster pace.

Here's a tip to remember: If you have a really tough decision to make, you have the option of requesting an additional 60 seconds, a feature that is offered on most sites.

You don't have to feel so rushed that you can't make an intelligent decision. You can take an extra moment or two to think things over and even after the time clock annoys you with its beep-beep, you can usually take at least 10 to 20 seconds more to make your decision.

Here's one other tip about playing online: Some online casinos protect a player if he gets disconnected and allow him to be declared all-in.

This means that he can win the chips that are in the pot at the time of his loss of connection, assuming that he has the best hand at the showdown. Any further bets after a player has been disconnected will be placed in a side pot among the remaining players. This procedure is used in regular casinos as well as online card rooms when a player has gone all in.

However, not all Internet card rooms allow this safety net. Some make you forfeit the hand if you get disconnected, so be sure you understand the rules of the online site. If you have an all-in protection, and have been forced to use it, make sure to request a new all-in protection option. Most online casinos will provide you with one upon request.

5. TAKE NOTES WHILE YOU'RE PLAYING

At most online poker rooms, there is a "notes" box that you can click. It's a handy little device where you can store your notes in a virtual filing cabinet.

Taking notes will help you determine the quality of your play, and give you a better idea of what the opposition is up to. Many times you will face different players, because players come and go with greater frequency online than they do in brick-and-mortar card rooms.

However, you often will find the same people playing at certain games and limits, and often at the same time of day. These are the types of players for whom you need your note-taking ability the most.

Just typing a few quick thoughts, such as "Joe Blow just played Q-4 suited in first position" can help you get a better idea about how your opponents play and the types of hands they enter the pot with. The more you know about your opponents, the better your chances of beating them.

6. LOOK FOR TELLS

A tell is a mannerism or gesture or some kind of movement that gives away the strength of a person's hand or what action he intends to take in the play of a hand. For example, Ed always stares straight at you when he is bluffing but he stares at the flop when he has a strong hand.

Hold on, I know you can't see your opponents when playing online like you can when playing face to face in a real casino, but that doesn't mean there are no tells to be discovered online. Let's take a look at a few of them.

Most sites have little spaces on the screen that say, "Fold to any bet," "Raise any bet," "Automatic check," or even

"Check and fold." For example, suppose you have seen the flop in a hold'em hand. You have flopped a pair, but are uncertain whether you have the best pair, so you decide to check.

If all the players who act after you rapidly check, that's a sign that they hit the automatic check button, which is usually a sign of weakness. This means that your pair is probably the best hand, at least for the moment, and you can consider betting it on the next round.

Other online players take a long time to act on their hands, and then come out betting or raising. For example, pay attention to the hands they show down when they take their time and you can figure out whether this hesitation is always done with a strong hand or not. If it always indicates a strong hand at the showdown, play accordingly.

If it doesn't always mean strength, then don't put too much importance on it. People who are playing online often are also doing something else at the same time, such as reading or answering e-mail, chatting with the other players, running to the bathroom, watching television, or any number of other things that could cause the delay. Pay close attention so that you can better decide whether the delays have any serious meaning.

7. PLAY SMALL TOURNAMENTS FIRST

If you're a tournament junkie like me, I suggest that you begin your online tournament career by playing the numerous online tournaments that are available around the clock. Tournament play is quite a bit different from cash game play. (The strategy differences are discussed in the tournament section of this book).

As a general rule, begin by playing small buy-in tournaments. Why? To create a comfort zone for yourself as a fledgling tournament aficionado.

If you do well in the smaller buy-in tournaments against weaker opponents, your confidence will steadily increase, and then you can think about stepping up. If you are successful in tournaments and learn to love them as I do, then you can increase the parameters of your comfort zone and play bigger buy-in events.

You will find tournaments you can enter for as little as $1 and as high as $530 on a regular basis, with all sorts of buy-ins in between those numbers. Some sites even offer freeroll tournaments in which the site puts up all the money for its customers.

I have seen as many as 5,000 players playing in the same freeroll tournament online. Whew, just try conquering that size field some time! Poker has a way of teaching all of us humility.

Playing small buy-in, one-table tournaments or one-table satellites online can be great learning experiences. For a limited investment, you can get a good idea about what kinds of hands people play and how they perform in different situations.

In all tournaments and satellites, you can't pull more money out of your pocket to buy more chips—if you lose your initial stack of chips you are out of action. Therefore, by playing small buy-in tournaments you limit your expenses and prevent yourself from spending more money than you planned on.

If you play a multi-table tournament and survive long enough, you will eventually wind up at the final table. Once you arrive at the championship table, the object is to win the tournament. To do this you must learn how to play with fewer and fewer players at the table.

Eventually it will get down to you and one other person. (Remember, the tournament doesn't end until one player has won all the chips.) One-table tournaments and satellites give you experience playing shorthanded, so you will have a much better feel for what to do when you make it to the final table of a multi-table tournament.

8. SCHEDULE YOUR TOURNAMENT PLAY

Because there are so many tournaments to choose from, you need to select the ones that suit your bankroll and your time requirements.

Don't sign up for a tournament that will take four hours to complete if you have to be somewhere else in two hours. Why bother to play in the first place if you don't have the time to finish it? If it's worth playing at all, then the tournament requires your best effort and enough free time to finish the job if you are lucky enough to go the distance.

I like to pencil in on my calendar the tournaments on the various sites that I am especially interested in. This way I can try to arrange my schedule to be available for as many of them as possible. I note the site, the game, the buy-in, the date, the starting time, and anything else that might be of interest. This type of planning is good discipline and makes good sense.

Many online poker rooms offer special promotions and tournament deals that are too good to pass up. By checking a site's upcoming events, I can choose the best bargains and put them on my tournament schedule.

I don't like ending my lists with "don't-do" items, but if you master these last two tips, you'll be on the fast track to playing winning online poker. Here comes my first "don't-do."

9. DON'T PLAY TO ESCAPE FROM SOMETHING ELSE

When you have a lot of other things on your mind, it is very difficult to focus on poker. If you've had an argument with somebody significant, it's hard to get it off your agenda so that you can concentrate and play your best game. If you insist on playing anyway, like so many of us often do, then at least play in a smaller game where you won't hurt your bankroll too much if you lose.

Above all, don't kid yourself into thinking that you can play a good game of poker, even though you're distracted or bothered by something. Even the best of players can't play their "A" game when they're stressed. Fortunately for the top players, even their "B" game or (gasp!) their "C" game is often better than most of the players they are competing against.

Most of us are best advised to either not play at all or play smaller limits than normal if we have too many problems or distractions. It's tough enough to win when you are focused and paying attention, so don't handicap yourself even more by playing when something is weighing heavily on your mind.

10. DON'T PUT MORE MONEY IN YOUR ONLINE ACCOUNT THAN YOU CAN AFFORD TO LOSE

This tip is ignored or forgotten more often than any of the other nine tips. Why? I think it's because, in the heat of battle, we often chase after our losses.

Sometimes we play higher than we should, other times we start playing bad poker—it's called going "on tilt" like the old-fashioned pinball machines used to do when they malfunctioned—and we wind up losing far more money than we should lose.

We start making bad choices in starting hands, chasing with the worst cards, calling or even raising when we should fold—you get the message.

Play within your financial comfort zone. Don't play in games that have bigger stakes than you can afford, or bigger stakes than you feel comfortable at playing.

I know a multimillionaire who can afford to play in the biggest games in Las Vegas, yet he isn't comfortable playing any higher than $20-$40 limit games. Then there's Bill Gates, the founder of Microsoft.

Gates has been known to step into a casino poker room from time to time where he usually plays three-six poker. That's $3-

$6, not 3-6 buildings or 3-6 oil wells like he could afford to play if he so chose.

Remember that once you have booked some wins, the money in your online account is real money—it spends just like money you earned at your job, and it is yours to keep or to reinvest.

Do not give it back and do not put more money in your online account that you can afford to lose. It is a big mistake to play with money that you need to put groceries on the table, or pay the rent or the doctor bills.

One way that you can avoid giving it back is quitting the game when you know you should. No matter how good the game, it's not a good game for you if you're losing. I use a very simple formula that governs when to quit the game. It is this: Never lose more in one session than you can reasonably expect to win in your next session. The formula assumes, of course, that you are playing the same form of poker at the same limits.

For example a good win in a $5-$10 game is around $200. If you are losing more than $200, which is 20 big bets, it's time to call it a day. Around 20 big bets is about the most you should ever lose in one session. You don't have to limit your wins, however. If you get $300 or $400 ahead in a $5-$10 game, and the game is still good and you're not too tired, by all means continue. The idea is to not limit your wins, but definitely limit your losses.

Other reasons to quit the game include being too tired to give it your best effort, realizing that your judgment is slipping. If you find yourself going on tilt because you've taken a few bad beats, it's time to leave. Another reason to quit is because some of the weaker players have left the game and have been replaced by much tougher opponents. If you think you are no longer a favorite to win in the game, for any reason, it's time to fold up your tent and hit the "I quit" button.

Shane's Review Questions

1. Why do you have to learn to play at a faster pace online than you play in a regular casino?

There are two reasons why online play is so much faster than brick-and-mortar casino. First, you get dealt about twice as many hands online in the same time frame as in a casino. Second, most online casinos use a time clock. If you take too long to act on your hand, you are forced to fold.

2. What is a useful online tell?

Online casinos have an automatic "check" button. If several players check very quickly, their fast checks "tell" you that none of them have a very strong hand. In that case, a single bet can sometimes win the pot for you.

3. What is the value of the "notes" box?

It's one way to learn a lot about your opponents' playing habits, as well as your own. When you're playing online, you can click on the notes box and type in your observations about your opponents. You also can note how you played and why, or perhaps type a question that about the play of a hand so that you can e-mail it to Tom McEvoy to get his expert opinion. In short, the notes box can be a useful learning tool.

4. Why start out playing small buy-in online tournaments when you could buy in with the big boys from the get-go?

First, your lessons will be considerably less expensive if you start small and build big. Further, if you aren't a computer whiz, playing small online tournaments will help you become accustomed to operating your computer and learning the finer points of playing online. Take on the little guys before you tangle with the big boys and your bankroll won't suffer nearly as many bruises.

5. What is a "comfort" zone?

Your comfort zone is the size of tournament or cash game that you can best afford and feel the most secure playing. You can get mighty nervous if you move out of that zone too early, especially before you have adequate experience and money to try a higher limit game. But if you've been successful at the lower limits and built your bankroll, you can expand your comfort zone and move on to greener pastures (as in "greenbacks") in a bigger game.

6. Why is it important to schedule your tournament play online?

Because there are so many online tournament to choose from. These days they seem to be multiply like bunny rabbits, so you need to pick the ones that best meet your time schedule and the ones you most want to play. Just always be sure to set aside enough time to play through to the end of the tournament—that is, if you really want to win it!

7. Why should you limit the amount of money you deposit in your online account?

Playing poker in cyberspace often seems as though you aren't playing real poker for real money. You don't have to get up from the table to buy more chips, and you don't have to cash out at the casino cage when you quit the game. It's just way too easy to keep adding money to the cyber table when you're losing.

But hey folks, it ain't Monopoly money you're playing with! Limit your loss potential by limiting the amount you have on deposit with your favorite online poker room.

How Would You Play This Hand?

PLAYING BIG CONNECTING CARDS AGAINST A SMALL POCKET PAIR

"I've been playing online tournaments for a while now, and I really prefer limit hold'em events because I'm a tight-aggressive player," Rich, a Canadian who regularly plays hold'em online, began his e-mail.

"Therefore, when I lose on the river, it usually doesn't cost me my stack. And if I make a bad call, I can usually bail out after the turn makes my hand worse!

"I've placed in the top five in multi-table tournaments three times now, and I've been in the money three other times. I feel that I am finally on the edge of making the next step to being a top contender regularly."

If Rich had ended his letter right there, I could've simply congratulated him on his success. But no winning streak goes without some punishment, as he found out in the next multi-table online tournament he played with a seventh-place finish.

He continued, "With two tables left, I was in first place with $34,000 in chips, and the lowest stack had $2,000. The player directly to my left had raised every time I had tried to limp into a pot.

Luckily, I had just knocked him out of the tournament after making a good call, hitting the nuts, and check-raising him all-in. In the very next hand I was the big blind and looked down at the K♦ Q♦. Only one player had called and the small blind had folded.

How Would You Play This Hand Before the Flop?
a. Just call
b. Raise

Here's How Rich Played It
"I decided I could finally limp into a pot safely. The player who had called had about $9,000 in chips and was in jeopardy of not making the final table.

The flop came down A♦ 10♦ 7♦! I had made the nut flush on the first three board cards."

How Would You Play This Hand on the Flop?

a. Bet and hope your opponent calls

b. Check with the intention of raising if your opponent bets

Here's How Rich Played It

"I checked, he bet, and I raised. He called. The turn was the 2♣. Again I bet, but this time he raised. I reraised him all in. He showed his 7-7 for a set and I showed my nut flush. You guessed it—the river brought the 2♥ to make a "boat" (a full house) for my all-in opponent, and I went from first to fifth place in a blink.

"I'm not sure there was any better way for me to have played this hand. I suppose I could have raised before the flop, but would he have folded pocket sevens in a limit tournament?

I guess I also could have bet the flush on the flop, but would he have laid down a set? He was only one more bet from being all in, so even if he was chasing, I figured he would go all in no matter what."

Tom's Analysis of Rich's Play

A single raise against a limper would not cause him to fold his pocket sevens. It didn't really matter how you played the hand after the flop—all the money was going in one way or the other. Your lucky opponent would not have ever folded a set on the flop heads-up, no matter what you did. I think you played it correctly after the flop. Just hope for better luck next time.

PLAYING Q-J IN A $22 ONLINE NO-LIMIT HOLD'EM EVENT

Online player Craig was playing a $22 buy-in no-limit hold'em event against 230 opponents. After plowing his way through the field, he made it to the final table with an average chip stack. With only six players in contention for the gold and the glory, he was in fourth place with approximately $28,000 in chips.

The chip leader was sitting to his left with about $40,000 in chips. The blinds were at the $600-$1200 level with a $125 ante when he met an untimely demise.

"I was on the button with a suited Q-J," Craig began. "Everyone passed to me on the button. The big blind hadn't been defending his blinds often, and the small blind (the chip leader) seemed to have tightened up his play waiting for a few more people to get eliminated. Neither player had seen a flop for several rounds."

How Would You Play This Hand Before the Flop?

a. Fold to preserve your chip count

b. Just call the size of the big blind

c. Raise to try to knock out the blinds and win the pot

Here's How Craig Played It

"Although Q-J suited isn't a big hand, I felt that a raise was in order to try to pick up the blinds and antes. I raised to $3,600, three times the big blind. The small blind called my raise, as did the big blind called as well.

"I wasn't happy with that result at all, but I did have position on both opponents and felt that if the flop didn't hit me hard, I could still get away from the hand. The flop came down K-10-9 rainbow. I had flopped the nut straight!

"I couldn't believe my eyes when the chip leader moved all in from the small blind. The big blind pondered and finally folded. And then it was my turn to act."

How Would You Play This Hand on the Flop?

a. Call with the rest of your chips because you have no worse than a tie with the chip leader

b. Fold because the chip leader might have flopped a set and you will be out of action if the board pairs and he wins the hand

Here's How Craig Played It

"Obviously I pushed the rest of my chips into the pot. The cards were turned over and the chip leader had a K-J offsuit. I was just hoping a queen didn't come off, because I wasn't interested in sharing a pot this size.

"Sure enough, I got my wish. A queen didn't come off, but something worse did. The turn brought a king and the river brought a jack, giving my opponent a full house!

"I was pretty disgusted with the outcome of the hand, but although I was disappointed and felt unlucky, I like to analyze every hand that busts me out of a tournament to see if there was any way I could have played the hand differently to avoid getting beat. After the flop there was no way to get away from my hand, but I wonder if my pre-flop play was flawed?

"Once the final table gets shorthanded, my raising standards usually drop. This table was playing pretty tight, and I was having success picking up the occasional pot without any struggle.

"When I showed down a hand, it was usually a big hand, and I think most of my opponents respected my raises.

"My question is, do you think raising with my Q-J suited was a mistake? If not, was the amount of my raise too small?

The small blind may have folded the K-J if I made a bigger raise, but I didn't want to get committed to a hand like Q-J pre-flop, so I raised an amount that I thought would make the blinds fold and also an amount that I could live with losing if one of them reraised. What do you think, Tom?"

Tom's Analysis of Craig's Play

In a shorthanded game in which the players in the blinds appear to be playing too tight, your button raise of three times the size of the big blind was correct. The chip leader actually should have folded his hand in the small blind.

But he must have had more gamble in his veins than you thought he had because he chose to gamble with you before the flop.

And on the flop, he apparently thought that taking a chance with his top pair and an inside straight possibility was worth the risk of moving all in.

There was no way to avoid this unpleasant result, unless you had folded before the flop. I believe you made the right play under the circumstances.

Hold'em Tournaments: The Big Money Game

The Basics of Tournament Play

Casinos and Internet poker rooms offer several types of tournaments. Most low-limit casino tournaments are **rebuy** events. In a rebuy tournament you can buy more chips during the first three **levels** of play (a prescribed period of time during which the size of the blinds remains the same) and you can make one final rebuy (an **add-on**) at the end of the rebuy period.

The majority of high-stakes tournaments are **freezeout** events. In a freezeout tournament, you cannot buy more chips. When you have lost your starting stack of chips, you must give up your seat in the tournament.

Another type of tournament is a **satellite**, a preliminary tournament that you can play to earn an entry into the main event. Satellites cost much less to enter than the main event and are an inexpensive way to buy in to a tournament that has a big entry fee. Most players who enter the World Series of Poker $10,000 championship tournament earn their buy-ins by winning a satellite that costs from $40 up to $1,000.

Whereas cash games are designed to keep players in the game, tournaments are designed to knock them out of the game. The purpose of a tournament is to eliminate contestants until only one player has won all the chips.

Unlike cash games, in which the blinds remain the same throughout the duration of the game, the blinds increase at regular intervals during a tournament.

Each interval is called a **level**, during which the blinds remain constant for 20 minutes, 30 minutes, an hour, or whatever time frame the tournament sponsor has designated. When a new level begins, the blinds increase by 50 percent up to 100 percent, depending upon the design of the tournament.

The design of a tournament is referred to as its **structure**. A tournament's structure includes such factors as the number of chips each player receives at the start of the event, the size of the blinds at the start of the tournament, whether rebuys are allowed, the length of each level, and the percentage of increase in the blinds from one level to the next.

Some tournaments are structured to end quickly. For example, satellites are fast-moving tournament events. Other tournaments, such as the World Series of Poker, World Poker Tour events, and the championship event in other major tournaments are structured to last a long time and give players plenty of time to play.

Before you enter a tournament, ask the following questions. The answers will help you design your tournament strategy.

How much is the buy-in?

The buy-in is often $20 to $40 for low-limit casino tournaments. In addition to that, the casino usually charges an entry fee (called the **vig**) to cover the house expenses for running the tournament. The usual entry fee in low-limit tournaments is about 15 to 20 percent of the buy-in. Sometimes

268

the entry fee is included in the buy-in amount, and is simply subtracted from the total prize pool of the tournament.

Is this tournament a rebuy event or a freezeout?

If you're playing a freezeout event, you need only the amount of the entry fee plus the vig. If you're playing a rebuy tournament, bring enough money with you to make several rebuys.

How much do rebuys and add-ons cost and when can I make them?

Any time you have fewer chips in your stack than you had in your starting stack, you can buy more chips, but only for a limited time.

You usually can rebuy only during the first three rounds of play (the **rebuy period**). At the end of the rebuy period, most rebuy events allow you to buy additional tournament chips, an add-on, for the same price you would pay for a rebuy.

What is the usual pay-out?

The amount of the pay-out is determined by the number of entries. Tournament directors keep records and can tell you the average amount of money that the winner usually wins. I always like to know how much I will earn if I win so that I can keep my "eyes on the prize," as the old saying goes.

How many places are paid?

The number of players who get paid usually depends on the number of entries. Small daily tournaments in hometown card rooms might pay only the final three players, while others reward the last five players in action. Tournaments with 100 entries usually pay everyone at the last table, and larger events pay two or more tables.

What percentage of the prize pool does each finalist receive?

The winning player usually gets 37 to 40 percent of the prize pool, with second place earning 20 to 25 percent and the remaining finalists dividing the rest of the money.

How long are the betting rounds?

In the majority of low-limit tournaments, the betting rounds are 20 minutes long, with a 15-minute break after the first hour of play.

How many chips will I receive to start with?

The lower the amount of the buy-in, the fewer chips you usually receive in your starting stack. If you enter a $20 buy-in event, you often will be given $200 in tournament chips. In a $1,000 buy-in tournament, you might start with $2,000 in chips.

What are the blinds in the first round of play?

In a low-limit tournament, the blinds often begin at $5-$10. The amount of the blinds in relation to the size of your starting stack of chips is an important indicator of how much "play" you will get for your money. Usually you want to receive at least 10 times the size of the big blind in your starting stack of chips.

How early should I be there to sign up?

Ask the tournament director in advance when tournament registration begins and whether he cuts it off at either a certain hour or after a designated number of players have paid their entry fees. I recommend arriving one hour before starting time for a Las Vegas tournament.

Which side games does the card room spread?

If you wash out of the tournament early, you'll probably want to play a cash game at which you excel. Be sure that the card room spreads your game of choice.

Tom's Top 10 Winning Tips

1. PLAY SMALL TOURNAMENTS TO START WITH

Very few players have the bankroll or the ability to be competitive in the big buy-in tournaments without first playing in the smaller ones. People who skip the smaller tournaments and go directly for the World Series of Poker or the World Poker Tour events are seldom successful to start with.

It takes lots of experience and practice to acquire the skills you need to compete on a level playing field with some of the best tournament players in the world. Fortunately, there are many small buy-in tournaments available both online and in brick-and-mortar casinos to choose from where you can practice and improve your tournament skills.

Playing in low buy-in tournaments can be a very inexpensive way to get the experience you need to move up the tournament ladder.

If you are successful and make money at the smaller buy-in events, you are usually ready to play in bigger events and face tougher competition. Most of us rise to the level of our competition.

Nobody in sports improved his performance by always competing against players of lesser ability. On the other hand, you can potentially lose a lot of money by playing in tournaments where the competition is too difficult for your level of play.

So what's the answer? I personally believe that playing in small buy-in tournaments online is the way to go. Online tournaments in every poker game imaginable are usually available around the clock. If you keep good records of your wins and losses, you will know when it's time to move up.

When your winning record over six months, for example, far exceeds your losses, try moving to a higher buy-in tournament where the competition is stiffer. Give the bigger buy-in tournaments two or three shots. If you feel comfortable competing at that level and believe you can become a winner, stay there for a while.

Then move up to an ever higher rung on the tournament ladder. But if you get slaughtered every time you put your buy-in on the butcher block, step back down the ladder until you have more experience and expertise under your belt.

2. MAKE GOOD CHOICES ON THE TOURNAMENTS YOU DECIDE TO PLAY

Here are some guidelines for how to select the best tournaments to play. First, making a good choice means playing within your bankroll and comfort zone. Don't gamble with the rent money playing a tournament that is too expensive for your budget. Second, you need to reserve the proper time commitment. Figure out how long it will take to play the tournament if you get to the final table and, hopefully, win it.

Make sure that you can be there mentally as well as physically for the duration of the tournament. If you will need to be somewhere else during the maximum length of time you think the tournament will require, skip that day's event, because your heart very likely will not be in it.

I play a lot of tournaments in casinos year around. Since I can't be everywhere at once, I choose the events that I most want to play and mark them on my calendar. I also keep close track of what days have the best online tournaments, noting the buy-in, the type of game, and what time the tournament starts. This helps me choose my best games at the time of day or night that is most convenient for me to play.

It is okay to schedule new games on your calendar, too, but just make sure that the cost of learning to play an unfamiliar tournament game is not too expensive. In other words, start small and work your way up if you like the game and are having some success with it.

3. DESIGN A TOURNAMENT STRATEGY

Like automobiles, tournaments come in many shapes and sizes. Depending on whether you like to drive in the slow lane or prefer the fast lane, you can play small tournaments with $20 buy-ins or less in casinos across the country any day of the week and 24-7 on the Internet—or you can take a shot at the granddaddy of them all by dragging $10,000 out of your pocket for a buy-in to the World Series of Poker.

And if you really want to live large, you can get a second mortgage on your home to post the $25,000 buy-in for the championship event of the World Poker Tour.

No matter what size tournament you enter, plan your strategy in advance as a sort of road map for your journey through the rounds of the tournament.

Most of the larger buy-in tournaments are freeze-out events that don't allow you to buy more chips when you go broke. If you lose all your chips, you're out of action. Rebuy tournaments give you a second chance when you lose your stack.

Most of the smaller tournaments—those with buy-ins of $20 to $100—allow you to rebuy for the first three rounds of the tournament and make one more rebuy (an **add-on**) at the end of the third round.

Freeze-out tournaments and rebuy events require somewhat different strategies. Generally speaking, you should play more conservatively in freeze-out tournaments, especially in the early rounds, than you play in rebuy events.

Most top players play very solid poker in freeze-out tournaments, entering pots only when they have good hands and are in good table position.

In rebuy tournaments, players usually play more loosely during the rebuy period (the first three rounds) than they do after the rebuy period has ended. At the end of the rebuy period, you'll often hear seasoned players say, "Now the *real* tournament begins!"

In other words, people play more solid poker when they know they can't buy more chips. Before you enter a rebuy event, you should decide how many rebuys you can afford and the conditions under which you will make them. For example, if you budget three rebuys and an add-on in a $20 rebuy tournament ($100 total), your strategy might include going all-in if you need to, rebuying if you lose that all-in pot, and adding on at the end of the rebuy period if weak players have the tall stacks.

The key to creating your own winning strategy is to plan your tournament strategy in advance—aggressive early, survival late, attack the short stacks, lay back with a low stack, and so forth.

Write your plan on the back of a business card and take it with you. Then stick with the plan for as long as it works for you.

Winning tips four and five will give you further advice on how to plan your strategy for rebuy and freeze-out events.

4. USE GOOD JUDGMENT IN DECIDING WHETHER TO REBUY AND ADD ON

If you plan to win a fixed percentage payout tournament (one that awards 30 percent of the prize pool to the winner, 15 percent to second, and so on) that allows rebuys, enter it with enough money to make rebuys and the optional add-on.

Some players plan to fire just one bullet—they intend to stick with their original buy-in only and quit if they lose it. This puts them at a disadvantage to their opponents who are willing to rebuy.

In most rebuy events, you will need to take advantage of the rebuy or add-on options to get to the final table. Your chip position, your budget, and the strength of the players who are in top chips status are determining factors in deciding whether you should add on at the end of the rebuy period.

If the casino awards bonus chips in addition to the usual number of chips you would receive when you add on, you are almost always correct in taking the add-on. Or if buying the add-on will increase your chip position by 33 percent or more, take the add-on.

Should you plan to always rebuy when you go broke? Not necessarily. If I get broke late in the rebuy period just after the limits have risen, I will often quit rather than go for another rebuy. Why? Because the amount of chips that I will receive for my rebuy money is much smaller in relation to the higher limits.

For example, if I will receive $200 in chips for the rebuy when the blinds are $25-$50, those chips won't go nearly as far as they would have gone when the blinds were only $10-$20 in an earlier round. The bottom line is to use good judgment in your rebuy decisions. Ask yourself, "Will a rebuy at this stage of the tournament under these conditions be a good investment?"

5. PLAY MORE CONSERVATIVELY IN FREEZE-OUT TOURNAMENTS

In freeze-out tournaments, where no rebuys are allowed, you literally are frozen out of action when you run out of chips. You must survive with your original stack of chips and build it along the way if you are to have any hope of winning. Since the opening limits and blinds are fairly small in relation to the chips in play, I recommend a more conservative strategy during the early rounds of play.

One of my best pieces of tournament advice—for which I have been quoted numerous times in poker literature—is this: You must survive long enough in the tournament to give yourself a chance to get lucky.

What does it mean? Nobody ever won a tournament without getting lucky at some point. Getting lucky could mean that you made a flush when your opponent flopped trips, or that you had aces when another player had kings.

Or maybe your opponents missed their drawing hands and you won the pot with a low pair. No matter how it happens, you can't get lucky if you're not in it. And that is why I believe that knowing how to survive is such an important skill.

Survival skills are necessary to win, but learning these skills takes time and practice, plus a whole lot of patience. It isn't much fun to fold hand after hand, is it?

Waiting for the cards to turn in my favor, or waiting for the correct moment to make a play is not my idea of having a good time at the poker table. But as the saying goes, "You gotta do what you gotta do."

Oftentimes you see players make reckless bets and raises and play cards you would never dream of playing. Sometimes they get lucky for a while, but most of the time they crash and burn, usually sooner rather than later.

If these rammer-jammers do survive with large stacks of chips, they often forget that they need to slow down and preserve them. That's when they find out the hard way that they can lose them just as fast as they won them. There's no need for you to have to learn that lesson on your own—learn from their bad example and continue playing good poker all the way.

6. PLAY STRAIGHTFORWARD POKER IN LOW-LIMIT TOURNAMENTS

The value of deception decreases in low-limit tournament play for several reasons. First, many players, especially new players, do not pay attention to their opponents. Therefore any deceptive plays you try probably will go right past them.

Suppose you've been playing tight as a drum and decide to take advantage of your tight table image by raising under the gun with a mediocre hand. Your bluff probably will backfire because most of your opponents are oblivious to the fact that you haven't played a hand for a long time.

Second, the players at your table change frequently as people go broke and are replaced by new opponents. There is an inverse ratio between deceptive value and the number of times players are rotated to your table. Many times, too, your table will be broken down and you will move to another table with all new opponents.

Slow-playing your solid hands in order to get more value for them usually is not a good idea in low buy-in tournaments. Why? Because the pace is fast and you usually will get plenty of callers even if you bet a good hand strongly, especially in the early rounds when most of your opponents are playing loose poker.

Continue playing solid poker throughout the tournament rather than falling into the trap of playing loose just because you can rebuy if you go broke. You do not have to be a maniac to win a tournament. Sure, maniacs will win once in a while, but it is usually the solid, selectively aggressive players who wind up in the winners' circle.

7. KEEP TRACK OF YOUR STACK

Always be aware of your stack's status relative to the size of your opponents' stacks and your playing position at the table. For example, if you have a very low stack with an average hand in middle position, you should be more inclined to throw away your hand. Save your dwindling chips for a stronger hand in a later and more favorable playing position.

When you're in a strong chip status and good position at the table, play opportunistically—you should attack the small stacks with a raise when you have a playable hand, especially against opponents who are very tight players. And late in the tournament, especially at the final table, use your big stack as a weapon of mass destruction.

If your stack resembles a mole hill rather than the Matterhorn, you are often well-advised to use survival tactics, rather than going up against a tall stack that could knock you out of the tournament.

8. WATCH THE CLOCK

Many tournaments have a tournament clock somewhere in the room. This clock tells you what the current limits are, what time the next increase in limits will take place, and how much time is left in the round. It often will also note how many players started the tournament and how many are still left.

Sometimes the clock will determine your strategy, just like it does in a football game. With 45 seconds remaining in the first half, a team might try an onside kick designed to steal the football from the enemy. Similarly, with only two minutes left in the betting round, you might raise from the button with a medium-strength hand to try to steal the blinds or build the pot, hoping that other players call and you get lucky on the flop.

Think of the tournament as an apple pie that is divided into as many pieces as there are betting rounds. You sometimes need to time your moves according to the number of remaining pieces in the pie.

When you are in favorable position late in the betting round, for example, you may decide to play a reasonable drawing hand more aggressively than you would otherwise play it. Why? Because the betting limits will double within the next two hands, making such a draw twice as expensive to take.

"If you can win one pot at each increment, you can sustain yourself," advised "Bulldog" Sykes, whose low-limit tournament winning record was exemplary.

9. PLAY VERY SMART POKER LATE IN THE TOURNAMENT

Late in a tournament, you cannot always wait for a premium hand because the antes and blinds begin gobbling up your chips like Pac-Man. Neither can you afford to take high-risk draws or play aggressively to try to get maximum value for your hand.

Whether a play is smart or not-so-smart depends on four things: (1) the strength of your hand; (2) your comparative chip status; (3) the nature of your opponents; and (4) your philosophy about whether it is more important to arrive at the final table, even with minimal chips, or whether it is better to gamble with your short stack in an attempt to build up your stack for a better shot at the tournament's bulls-eye. In my opinion, you can't wait for the nuts or even a big hand. You have to take a shot with any playable hand and be aggressive with it. Not everybody agrees with me, of course.

Some tournament aficionados advise more conservative play, using survival tactics to arrive at the final table rather than risking taking a dive out of the tournament's money pool.

I prefer to play conservatively at the next-to-last table, for example, no matter what the size of my stack, because I love competing at the final table. I always feel that if I can just make it far enough, I too will have a shot at that brass ring.

10. KEEP YOUR COOL UNDER PRESSURE

The biggest tournament mistake a player can make is giving up hope. I have won hundreds of tournaments during my 25-year career as a tournament specialist—including the World Series of Poker championship—but I have never won a tournament without being in what looked like a hopeless chip position sometime during the event.

I waited for what I thought was the best hand or the best situation to put my last few chips in the pot. And I never gave up hope.

Don't throw your last chip in the pot simply out of desperation or frustration. Don't let other players distract you, or allow lady luck to demoralize you. After all, this is the only chance you'll ever get to win this tournament, today, right now.

Winston Churchill put it this way: "Never ever ever ever give up!" Shane and I have always loved that quote. I wonder if he played poker?

Shane's Review Questions

1. Why should most players start off by playing in low buy-in tournaments?

Low buy-in events are an inexpensive way to gain some tournament mileage under your belt before you try tangling with the big boys in higher buy-in tournaments. Old timers refer to it as "paying your dues" for membership in the winners' circle.

2. Why is a straightforward approach to poker the best strategy in low-limit tournaments?

Because most of the players in a low buy-in event are neither highly skilled nor very experienced. Therefore some of the bluffs and fancy plays that might work against better opponents will fall flat against beginners.

3. Why is your stack size so important in a tournament?

Chips are like soldiers in an army. The more chips you have, the better your chances of survival against the enemy, the more options you have in defending yourself against aggressive opponents, and the better your chances of winning each battle in the tournament war.

4. Suppose you are playing in the first round of a no-limit hold'em tournament and a player that you know nothing about makes a standard raise from first position. Everybody folds to you on the button. Your hand is the K♠ Q♠. What should you do?

Give your opponent more credit that he might actually deserve by assuming that he is a solid player who knows what he's doing.

In no-limit hold'em, a K-Q is a trouble hand that might trap you on the flop. Fold.

5. Why is a more conservative strategy usually the best approach during the early rounds in a freeze-out tournament?

Because you cannot buy more chips if you lose all the chips you started with. You must survive by preserving and building your original stack. Therefore you do not take a lot of risks with marginal hands.

6. Suppose you are playing a no-limit hold'em tournament with very aggressive players. Should you limp into pots with small pairs and suited connectors when you are in an early or middle position?

No, it is seldom correct to play these types of hands unless you are sitting in a late position and the pot has not been raised in front of you. Small pairs and connecting cards can burn up too many of your chips when you are play them from an early position because you often have to fold before the flop if somebody raises after you have acted.

7. Why is it so important to never, ever give up hope during a tournament?

Because it is always possible to make a big comeback from a dismal chip position. In fact many tournament winners, including Tom and me, have placed in the money after being so low on chips they were barely visible above the felt.

Be more patient than you are inclined to be, wait for the best hand or the best situation, and then push your Davids into the middle—they just might slay Goliath and send you to the winners' circle, where Tom and I hope to meet you one day soon.

A Tournament Question

"I recall reading that it is best to accumulate chips early in a tournament by being a little more aggressive," Ken, who plays a lot of low-limit casino poker tournaments, said in his e-mail. "But late in the tournament, I've read that you should play much tighter and let the other players knock each other out, provided that the blinds aren't eating you up. What's your opinion?"

Since I was out of town when Ken's e-mail arrived, I asked Shane Smith, author of *Poker Tournament Tips from the Pros*, to answer this important question.

Here is Shane's expert advice: "Yes, you want to increase your stack in the early rounds, but not at the risk of either busting out or investing more money on rebuys than the tournament is worth.

"It's always a dilemma, so I usually gauge my number of rebuys according to the size of the tournament and how the cards are running for me. If I'm running bad, I run for the door real early."

I agree with Shane's advice. But if you're playing in a freeze-out tournament, I also suggest following the advice of Linda Johnson, spokesperson for the World Poker Tour. "What does it take to get the money? When I first started playing, I played much tighter than I do now. Then I came to realize that you have to accumulate chips early. If you don't have them when the limits go up, you're in trouble. You might play a few more 'button' hands, especially in Texas hold'em tournaments. Plus, a few more marginal hands in the beginning that I never would have played in a tournament years ago.

"What you have to remember in tournament play is that in the beginning, you can see a flop for, say $20, but in two hours that flop is going to cost you $100. So you can see five flops now for the same price as one flop later on.

"You can lose all five $20 flops and still have some money left, but if you hit a few of them you'll have a lot of chips. I would rather play J-10 five times early on hoping to get lucky than wait for aces once, because I can't play that J-10 when the limits get very high. It gets to the point where you can't play those marginal hands because they cost you too much."

Linda is right. Here's what happens: In the beginning stage of the tournament, there are more multiway pots so you can come in with hands such as J-10 or 9-8 suited.

But in the later stages it's almost "raise or release." You're playing that J-10 against one or two people at the most who already have brought the pot in for a raise, so you couldn't possibly have the best hand. Your J-10 is not playable because you aren't getting the right price for it.

I hope these tips will help you build your stack on the way to the winner's circle.

A Tournament Tale

I believe that the following viewpoints and play-by-play analysis from Shane Smith, who "sweated" me (stood by and encouraged me at the final table) during the $500 buy-in limit hold'em tournament at the Queens Poker Classic VI, merits your attention. From here on out, it's her story.

Playing correct tournament strategy, especially near the end, pays off—not only in added money, but also in additional respect from opponents and railbirds alike.

Take last night at the *Queens Poker Classic VI*, for example.

Nestled among a gallery of around 40 other rooters, railbirds and reporters, I was sweating my tournament hero, Tom McEvoy, when the final nine began battle for the $500 limit hold'em title and top money of $45,000.

I had watched McEvoy struggle his way up the ladder from third table to second and finally to the last table with a chip count that was so small it was barely distinguishable from the felt. Weeks seemed to pass without his playing a hand while he was in his survival mode.

At the second table, three tall stacks busted out while McEvoy gingerly avoided the clutches of brutal bankruptcy and slowly built his miniscule stack. Each time an opponent bombed out of action, I figure that his conservative tactics earned him an additional $200 or so. But he was not the only one playing superior survival poker—two other players also used it to increase their earnings at the last table.

At midnight, the final table assembled with Dr. Ray Warchaizer leading the pack with a commanding chip stack of $32,000, and New Yorker Bill Seymour (the eventual winner) trailing in second place with $18,000. McEvoy was a straggler with only $11,500.

When it got down to six-way action, Doug Saab used a tournament tactic that brought laughter (which so often defuses final table tension) from his opponents, and applause from the rest of us.

With only $7,000 in chips left, Saab had posted the $4,000 big blind, leaving him with $2,000 to meet the small blind, plus one extra $1,000-chip. He mucked his big-blind hand against a late-position raiser

306

and awaited the small blind's imminent arrival.

A player raised, as they usually do in almost every pot at the final table, leaving Saab with the option of throwing in his last chip in a hail-Mary attempt to win the pot, or saving it for the next hand when he would be on the button.

Looking two seats to his left, he could see Steve Kopp, who had only one chip left with the big blind hovering over him like a vulture. Leaning forward with an "I'll let you take your chances" smile on his face, Saab counted down his competitor and then deftly threw away his hand to the knowing laughter of the table and the appreciative applause of the gallery—but to the chagrin of Kopp.

We all knew that the laydown possibly could earn Saab an additional $1,700, the difference between the fifth and sixth place payoffs. Alas for Saab, Kopp opted to play his next hand (J-8) from first position, rather than waiting to post that lonesome chip in the big blind. He won the pot when he high-carded the opposition and then went on to survive both his blinds.

Although Saab had used proper tournament strategy in conserving his case chip, he finally busted out in sixth place a few hands later. Shortly thereafter, his brief, three-hand winning streak spent, Kopp finished fifth. Both men had shown tournament class, playing superior strategy from precarious positions in their efforts to climb up a rung on the payout ladder.

During the short break before the final-table action began, I asked McEvoy what his strategy would be. "Just like I talk about in Championship Tournament Poker—play selectively aggressive," he said. Earlier I had seen him aggressively raise

Warchaiser with an A-K and win the pot with an unpaired, high-card hand.

"He'd been playing too many hands," McEvoy explained, "and I thought that he was trying to run over me."

Unfortunately, he selected a Q-10 on the button for aggression against Chinese poker specialist Andy Bloch, who also had been playing a crafty game of dodge-the-bullet poker, and who was sitting in the big blind with A-10.

When a 10 came on the flop followed by a second one on the turn, McEvoy pushed in most of his chips only to lose them to Bloch's higher kicker. Unable to recover from such massive damage to his stack, McEvoy was the next man out in fourth place, winning $7,377 for his evening's labor.

The crowd applauded in appreciation of his fine work and his opponents seemed to sigh in relief as the 1983 World Champion dragged his weary body from the table at 1:00 A.M. As a fan darted over to ask him for an autograph, I announced "Size medium!" anticipating that McEvoy would reward me for my sweating duty with the signature jacket that all last-table finishers receive.

I play many low-limit poker tournaments around Las Vegas, but as yet they have not educated me (nor thrilled me) nearly as much as watching and sweating and analyzing and cheering the final-table action at the major tournaments I have attended.

Mastering how to survive with a short stack for over five hours as McEvoy did; comprehending how to move up the pay scale by either saving that last chip or by investing it wisely as his opponents did; and learning how to endure the up-and-down luck of the tournament see-saw: These are the lessons that count, the skills that make the difference where it matters the most—in the bank.

How Would You Play This Hand?

LITTLE CARDS WIN A BIG POT IN A LIMIT HOLD'EM TOURNAMENT

Knowing that some players (not you or me, of course) sometimes search more ardently for reasons to play than for reasons to fold, I found the following letter particularly interesting.

Let me explain in advance, however, that this player is very perceptive and posed his end question to satisfy his curiosity about whether he made the correct play in a tricky situation, one that was further complicated by the presence of a friend with "attitude" against whom he was competing.

He also is someone who genuinely tries to learn from his mistakes, a personal trait that I admire in anyone. Decide for yourself what you would have done had you been in his boots.

"I discovered poker about two years ago and have been playing quite regularly in local cash games and tournaments," Ron explained.

"Only recently have I overcome the 'steam mode' when I make mistakes or take an ugly beating. I now try to view all my disappointments as learning experiences for my future pay days." (Right on! This is the way that all potential winners view their *faux pas*.)

"Happily, I now am finishing in the money more often than not in tournament play," he continued. "I'd like to get your advice on a disturbing situation that I recently encountered during a limit hold'em tournament that promised a big payoff to the winner.

"We were down to the last two tables and a friend of mine and I both were in tough spots with the blinds at $750 and $1,500. My buddy had about $2,900 in chips and I had $4,500 at the break. I was five away from the big blind and knew that I was going to have to play aggressively as soon as the cards were in the air again.

"Sure enough, as soon as the break was over, four players checked to me and I immediately raised to $3,000 to try to win the blinds. I had a K-J but even if it had been a 7-2, I was coming out strong. I won the blinds.

"On the next three hands I did the same thing and again won the blinds. One in front of the button with a Q-10, I made the same play and was called only by the big blind.

"He held pocket sevens and they stood up. I trashed my hand and my friend immediately stood up from across the table and asked the dealer to roll over my mucked hand for everyone to see.

"The dealer obliged and turned it over. No doubt the other people at the table were curious and skeptical as to what I was raising with at that point.

"Two hands later, I was the big blind and was dealt the 5♥ 2♥. It was checked all the way to my friend who raised all in for $2,900. Everybody folded all the way around to me. I had a decision to make. At this point the pot held $5,150 in chips and I reviewed the situation in my mind.

"We're heads-up, he's all in, and there are no other callers, I thought, so my stack cannot get hurt for more than the $1,400 that it will take for me to call the raise. And I'll still have $7,600 even if I lose this pot. I'm still not at a safe chip level as the blinds will be doubling to $1,500-$3,000 the next round. If I get lucky and rags or hearts fall, I'll have some breathing room. After all, I've never won a tournament without taking some chances."

How Would You Play This Hand Before the Flop?

a. Fold because you have a marginal hand

b. Call your friend's all-in bet to try to win the pot

Here's How Ron Played It

"I called. As it turned out, I paired my deuce to win the pot. My buddy trashed his hand and stormed out of the poker room. He was so mad he didn't even play the next day's no-limit hold'em tournament for which he already had registered.

My question is: Did I have any common-sense justification for making this call, or was I just in ram-and-jam mode and looking for an excuse to call?"

Tom's Analysis of Ron's Play

In my opinion, Ron, you made a borderline decision when you called the raise. However, since you already had $1,500 in the pot, plus $750 from the small blind, plus your opponent's $1,400 raise, and it was going to cost you only $1,400 more to call, you were getting about the right price (the proper pot odds) to play this hand, plus you had a lot of chips in your stack.

It doesn't sound as though your opponent (friend?) had an overpair but rather was steamed up at you and tried to raise you out of your blind as a revenge tactic for your having raised his blind earlier.

In this situation, he wouldn't necessarily need to have a big hand or a big pair to raise. Even if he didn't have a big hand, you still needed to at least pair up to hope to win the pot.

The only hand that you are a huge underdog against in a situation like this is an overpair, so if your opponent has only two random high cards, for example, you're getting enough pot odds to justify the call. If you had had fewer tournament chips than what you had, I would have suggested that you fold the hand.

But since you had $9,000 in chips to work with, even if you took the small blind and passed you still would have had just a shade less than $7,000 in chips with enough time to pick up another potentially winning hand before you had to post the blind again.

Although your call was marginally acceptable, I agree that you may have been in the ram-and-jam mode. In other words, you were looking for an excuse to call rather than a reason to fold. By the way, are you sure that this guy really is your friend? In your situation I might want to rethink my friendship with someone who is a hothead and a steamer.

WHEN THE CHIP LEADER IS PASSIVE IN A LIMIT HOLD'EM TOURNAMENT

Some players believe that their toughest opponents at the tournament table are players like Phil or T.J. or Annie—you know, the seasoned champions with bracelets up to their elbows—but that isn't always the case. Sometimes it's that passive limper sitting in seat eight who causes you the most headaches. Emailer Alan ran into just such a "Meek Marvin" in a limit hold'em tournament he recently played.

"One of the players at my table gave me a good deal of trouble," he began. "He was a perennial limper with loose standards for starting hands who tended to passively call after the flop.

"In live games, players like him are my bread and butter, but with a short stack in a tournament, it's another matter. With blinds of $30-$60 and a stack size of $400, I figured that I had to be choosy about the hands that I played, and I wanted to be able to steal my fair share of the blinds.

"The trouble was that the limper seated across the table from me made stealing next to impossible. If I'd had a deep stack, there would have been plenty of hands with which I would happily have trailed in after him in the hopes of hitting a few flops. But with my stack size I was unhappy about committing a significant fraction of my chips to such gambles. How would you recommend playing in this situation?"

Tom Analysis of Alan's Strategy

Good question, Alan. What *do* you do when you're playing in a tournament against a loose passive player who plays a lot of hands, calls raises with marginal cards, *and* has a lot of chips?

You simply have to wait for a better starting hand with which to attack him. You can't afford to mix it up with marginal starting hands against this type of guy because he is virtually bluff-proof.

Occasionally however, I'll be so short-stacked that I simply must play a marginal hand against this type of player and hope that it wins. You are correct in feeling unhappy about committing a significant portion of your chips in these types of situations. These players are always dangerous when they have lots of chips because they are unpredictable. When you're in a multiway pot with them, they are less of a factor because you're not fighting them alone.

Meek Marvin is especially dangerous shorthanded when you're trying to isolate against only one other player because he keeps calling and getting in your way, in contrast to Maniac Mike who keeps raising and getting in the way. Eventually both types usually self-destruct.

Alan's Next Strategy Question

"I hunkered down and waited for superior cards that never came, but in retrospect I think that I was playing too tightly. At one point, the limper and one other player were in the pot for one bet each. I held a K-9 offsuit in late position. Should I have played it or folded?"

How Would You Play This Hand Before the Flop?

a. Fold

b. Call

c. Raise

Here's How Alan Played It

"I didn't want to commit nearly 10 percent of my stack with a marginal hand, and I sure didn't want to get trapped into playing the hand for two bets in the event that a player after me had a real hand and raised, so I mucked it."

Tom Analysis of Alan's Play

Alan was correct in folding. K-9 is simply too marginal a hand to play against two or more limpers.

Alan Asks about How to Play Against Passive Players

"Normally I don't open a tournament pot for one bet. I either raise or fold. But suppose that I have one of the larger stacks at a table where some players are beginning to get desperate. If I limp from early position with some hands that I ordinarily would fold (small suited connectors like 6-5), then the small stacks who might be tempted to steal with a hand like A-7 or K-3 would be deterred.

"In that case I could see the flop cheaply with some marginal hands and maybe win an occasional big pot. It seems to me that this play could be especially useful close to the bubble, particularly in hands when another big stack is taking the blinds. Do you think that this strategy makes sense?"

Tom's Answer to Alan's Final Question

No, it doesn't make good sense or good poker. If you did that, you would be lowering your game to the level of your opponents. You'd be playing their game, not yours. Playing hands such as 6-5 is a good way to destroy your big stack, not increase it.

You're giving smaller stacks the chance to double through you and medium stacks a chance to hurt you. The medium stacks can then build themselves while you're tearing down your stack and pretty soon, guess what? You're looking eye to eye.

You would be screwing things up big-time if you started limping in with K-9 and 6-5, that kind of garbage.

Alan, the sooner you get Meek Mike off your mind and start playing *around* him, not *into* him, the sooner you and

I can share the glory and the gold in the winner's circle.

POCKET JACKS SQUARE OFF AGAINST A-Q IN A SMALL NO-LIMIT HOLD'EM TOURNAMENT

Sometimes players in no-limit hold'em will overbet the pot to protect a weak hand. Other times they overbet it because they are inexperienced at the game. By **overbetting the pot**, I mean that the raiser raises an amount of money that is disproportionate to the size of the blinds.

This type of big-chip bet can put an opponent with a medium to strong hand in a quandary as to whether to call, fold or reraise, a predicament in which Hal recently found himself. Here is the scenario that he emailed to me.

"The following situation occurred while I was playing in a small, four-table, no-limit hold'em tournament with a $40 buy-in and unlimited rebuys for $35 each during the first hour of play," Hal began.

"I have just made the final table and have about $8,000 in chips in front of me while the chip leader has about $21,000. The blinds are $200-$400.

"First prize is about $1,900 and second is about $1,200. Even though only four places are officially awarded prizes, a settlement often takes place among the last five or six remaining players at the final table.

"I haven't been running well and have nosed my way into about sixth or seventh place by virtue of getting out of the way of other players, stealing blinds, and drawing out on two occasions.

"Now I am in the big blind with pocket jacks, only my second big pair of the evening. All the players fold between me and the chip leader, who is sitting in a middle position. He raises $6,000. Everybody else folds to me."

How Would You Play This Hand?
    a. Fold

    b. Call

    c. Raise all in

Here's How Hal Played It

"I went all in. Without hesitation he called with an A-Q offsuit. The flop came Q-Q-6 followed by blanks on the turn and river. I was busted, dammit!

"When I presented this hand to players whose opinions I value at my club, half said that I had a small advantage and should either have called or, better yet, folded. The other half believed that I did the right thing in going all in.

"In retrospect, I now wonder whether I should have folded, figuring I could save chips and wait for better position knowing that I probably could squeak into the money or maybe even have a run at the top three spots. Did I make the correct play?"

Tom's Analysis of Hal's Play

The answer to that question depends upon your answer to this question: "What are my goals in this tournament?" If you're looking to edge up into the money, passing is the correct play. In other words, if you want to try to lock up a money spot, you can fold and wait for a better situation.

However, all my instincts cry out to play this hand by moving all in because (1) I'm trying to win the tournament, and (2) I think the chip leader's hand is somewhat weak.

Why do I think he's weak? Because when he overbet the pot by putting in $6,000 when the blinds were only $200-$400, he's telling me that he has a hand he doesn't want anybody to call and he's trying to protect it by overbetting the pot. Win, lose or tie, I believe that you made the right play when you moved all in.

J-J AGAINST 10-9 IN A BIG NO-LIMIT HOLD'EM TOURNAMENT

It's great to flop a set in hold'em, but sometimes a higher set or even a lesser drawing hand will sink your prized trips. It's happened to even the best tournament players, and it happened to Joe, who was playing a big no-limit hold'em tournament in Southern California.

With five tables remaining and the blinds at $200-$400 in the championship event, Joe found himself on the button with pocket jacks. The final 18 players would be receiving a payday, and he had about $5,500 in tournament chips.

"A wild player sitting in first position raised and made it $2,000 to go," Joe wrote in his e-mail. "He had developed a betting pattern that was easy to read. He would make a fairly large raise when he had nothing and a small raise when he had a high pocket pair or A-K. His crazy play had been holding up and he had about $10,000 in chips, since he seemed to always get there with trash hands."

How Would You Play This Hand Against A Raise?

    a. Raise

    b. Fold

    c. Call

    d. Reraise

Here's How Joe Played It

"I called his $2,000 raise. The flop came K-Q-J rainbow, giving me a set of jacks. My loose opponent bet $1,000 and I came over the top of him, moving in with my remaining $3,500 in chips.

He called and showed me a 10-9 offsuit. The board never paired and he won with the straight, sending me straight out the door."

Tom's Analysis of Joe's Play

Thinking the hand through after his untimely exit, Joe thought that maybe he had done something wrong. "I think I might have had two better options than the play I chose to make," he continued.

"(1) I could have just folded and kept attacking the smaller stacks like I had been doing to advance my chip position; or (2) Since I was sure that he had a weak hand, I could've made a substantial raise, possibly even an all-in raise, before the flop to try to make him drop his hand."

First of all, the worst possible option against this type of player is to flat call. I don't like your call at all. In this scenario, calling costs you $2,000 in chips, leaving you with $3,500. In this case, you might as well just gamble with the rest of it and go all in. Why? Because you won't be in very good shape if you lose the hand.

I also think that if you had raised all-in, you would have had an excellent chance to move your opponent off his hand and cause him to fold it. Even a loose-aggressive player will lay down a hand when he thinks that he is clearly beaten.

Your true options are either to fold or move all in. Since your opponent was a loose player and had made a substantial bet before the flop, clearly the move-in bet would have been the superior play by far.

When you move in, you don't have to second-guess yourself in the event that he calls. If he calls an all-in raise with a 10-9 before the flop, he's even more of a maniac than you thought he was!

But by allowing him to see the flop with no additional damage to his stack, you gave him a chance to draw out on you—and indeed he did. Even though the flop seemed to be favorable for you, it cost you a chance to cash in the tournament.

Remember that you have to play the player just as much as you play your hand, particularly in no-limit hold'em. One way to handle a wild player is to come over the top of him. Another way to handle a maniac is to simply get out of his way.

But in your situation, two jacks is too tough a hand to either fold or just call with, even against a wild, aggressive player.

Therefore, I would've moved in on this player and tried to win the pot right there. That way, at least I would know that I had substantially the best of it and that he made a mistake by calling. As it turned out, you are the one who made the mistake.

In fact, tournament poker is a game of mistakes. So often, you can play perfect tournament strategy deep into the tournament, then make one or two mistakes, and be forced to head for the rail rather than the roses.

Glossary

Glossary

Act. The action you take in the play of a hand—fold, call, raise or reraise. "Since I was the last player to *act* and everybody had folded, I decided to raise."

Add-on. The last opportunity players have to buy chips in a rebuy event. "I *added on* at the end of the rebuy period to beef up my stack."

Any ace. An ace with a weak kicker (A-7 or A-5, for example). "Some people will play *any ace* from late position in a tournament."

Backdoor a flush/straight. Make a hand that you were not originally drawing to by catching favorable cards on later streets. "I had been betting top pair, but when a fourth spade hit at the river, I *backdoored* a flush."

Beat into the pot. When an opponent bets an inferior hand, you gladly push your chips into the pot. "When three clubs came on the flop, Chris moved in. I *beat him into the pot* with my ace-high flush."

Behind (Sitting). To have the advantage of acting after someone else acts. "So long as you're sitting *behind* the other players, you have the advantage of position."

Big ace. An ace with a big kicker (A-K or A-Q). "When the flop came A-6-2, I played my *big ace* strong."

Big blind. The larger of two forced bets; usually twice the size of the small blind. "Every time I was the *big blind*, Hank raised on the button and forced me to fold."

Big flop. The flop comes with cards that greatly enhance the strength of your hand. "I caught a *big flop* that gave me the nut flush."

GLOSSARY

Board (The). The five community cards that all the players use to make their best possible hand. "I make a flush when the *board* came with three cards in my suit."

Boss hand. A hand that is the best possible hand. "When you have the *boss hand*, you should bet it as aggressively as possible, especially if you think your opponents have drawing hands."

Bully. Play aggressively. "When I have a big stack in a tournament, I like being able to *bully* the entire table."

Button. A small round disk that indicates which player gets to act last on a particular hand. "Everybody folded to me on the *button*, so I raised the pot to try to steal the blinds."

Buy-in. The amount of money it costs to enter a tournament. The cost of the buy-in is often used to describe the size of a tournament. "He didn't have enough money for the *buy-in* to the $1,000 hold'em event, so he sold shares of his action to three other players."

Case chips. Your last chips. "He raised all in with his *case chips*."

Change gears. Adjust your style of play from loose to tight or from tight to loose; from aggressive to passive or from passive to aggressive. "Passive Paul *changed gears* late in the tournament and raised four pots in a row."

Check-raise. To check when you are the first player to act so that you can raise if another player bets. "When Louise *check-raised* me from first position, I knew she had a strong hand, so I folded."

Chip status. How the number of chips you have in front of you compares to those of your opponents. "Looking around the table, I realized that I was the lowest in *chip status*—I had to win some chips right away or I'd be out of the tournament."

Cold call. Call a raise without having put an initial bet into the pot. "Cloutier raised, Hellmuth reraised, and I *cold called*.

Come over the top. Raise or reraise. "I raised it $2,000 and Sexton *came over the top* of me with $7,000."

Cutoff seat. The seat immediately to the right of the button. "He raised from the *cutoff seat* to try to shut out the button and the blinds."

GLOSSARY

Early position. The first two or three seats to the left of the big blind. "I wanted to gamble with my 8-7, but realized that I shouldn't play it because I was in *early position*."

First position. The first player sitting to the left of the big blind. "My dad told me that I should never play weak cards like 10-9 or pocket fives from *first position*."

Flat call. To call a bet without raising. "When he bet in to me, I just *flat called* because I had a straight draw and wanted to see the next card cheaply."

Flop (The). The first three community cards that the dealer places face-up in the center of the table. "I tried to hide my excitement when I made trip aces on *the flop*."

Flop to it. The flop cards enhance the value of your hand. "If you don't *flop to it*, you can get away from the hand."

Freeze-out tournament. When your original buy-in is gone, you cannot rebuy or add on extra chips to remain in play. "All World Poker Tour events are *freeze-out tournaments*."

Get away from it. Fold, usually what appeared to be a premium hand until an unfavorable flop negated its potential. "If you don't flop to your hand, *get away from it*."

Get the right price. The pot odds are favorable enough for you to justify calling a bet or a raise with a drawing hand. "Since I was *getting the right price*, I called the bet with an open-end straight draw."

Isolate. To raise or reraise to limit the action to yourself and a single opponent. "I raised on the button to *isolate* against the big blind."

Increment. The increase in chips required to post the blinds and antes at the start of a new level (round) in a tournament. When the blinds rise from $25-$50 to $50-$100, the increment has doubled. " I knew the *increments* would double on the next hand, so I decided to raise with my Q-10 on the button."

Jammed pot. The pot has been raised the maximum number of times and may also be multiway. "You should pass with a weak hand if the *pot has been jammed* before it gets to you."

Key card. The one card that will make your hand a winner. "I knew that I needed to catch a 10, the *key card* to my straight draw."

GLOSSARY

Key hand. A hand that turns the tide of fortune in a tournament. "The *key hand* that put me in a position to win came when I hit my flush at the river and won a huge pot."

Late position. The button and one or two seats to the right of the button. "Tom told me that I could raise with a Q-J suited when I'm in *late position* and nobody else has entered the pot."

Lay it down. Fold. "I knew I was beaten so I had to *lay down my hand* when Doyle raised.

Level. The length of time that a tournament stays at a certain betting limit before the blinds increase. Also referred to as a round. "During the first *level* of a freeze-out tournament, you should play solid hold'em strategy."

Limp. Enter the pot by just calling. "I decided to just *limp* in with a pair of tens and see the flop as cheaply as possible."

Limper. A player who enters the pot for the minimum bet. "When there are two *limpers* already in the pot, a pair of jacks should be your minimum raising hand."

Make a deal. Negotiate a new way of dividing the money among the top finishers at the last table in a tournament. "There was so much money in the prize pool and they were so close in chip status, the three finalists decided to *make a deal* and just split the prize money evenly."

Make a move. Try to bluff. "When the board paired sixes, Max *made a move* at the pot. I thought that he was bluffing but I had nothing to call him with."

Middle position. The fourth, fifth, sixth and seventh players to act after the big blind in a 10-handed game. "Since I was in a *middle position* at the table, I thought that I could safely play my K-J offsuit."

Nut draw (The). You have a draw to the best possible hand. "When two clubs come on the board and you have the A♣ J♣, you have *the nut flush draw*."

Nuts (The). The best hand possible at the moment. "Remember that you can flop *the nuts* and lose it on the turn; for example, when you flop the nut straight and the board pairs on the turn making a full house for your opponent."

Offsuit. Cards that are not suited. "Even though three suited cards were showing on the board, nobody made a flush, so Jeremiah won the pot by making a straight with his Q-J *offsuit*."

Out (An). A card that completes your hand. "When the board came with the Q-J-10 of spades, I was holding the ace of spades and knew that my only *out* for making a royal flush was the king of spades."

Out of position. Playing marginal hands such as small pairs and medium connectors from early position. "I wanted to play my pocket fours, but I knew that I was *out of position* and could get raised, so I folded."

Overpair. To have a pair in your hand that is higher than the highest card showing on the board. "When the board came Q-J-6, I had an *overpair* with my pocket kings."

Pass. Fold. "When Ron raised in front of me, I decided to *pass*."

Pay off. To call an opponent's bet at the river even though you think that he might have the best hand. "When the board paired at the river, I decided to *pay him off* when he bet."

Payout. The prize money you win at the end of the tournament. "The *payout* for first place was $500, but the payout for third place was only $100."

Play back. Responding to an opponent's bet by either raising or reraising. "If a tight opponent *plays back* at you, you know he probably has the nuts."

Play fast. Aggressively betting a drawing hand to get full value for it if you make it. "Many players *play fast* in the early rounds of rebuy tournaments to try to build their stacks."

Play slow. The opposite of playing fast. You wait to see what develops before pushing a hand. "When you make the nut straight on the flop and there's a chance that a flush draw is out or possibly a set, why not *play your hand slow* to start with?"

Play with. Staying in the hand by betting, calling, raising or reraising. "You should realize you're going to get *played with* most of the time because hold'em is a limit-structure game."

Put on the heat. Pressuring your opponents with aggressive betting strategies to get the most value from your hand. "You might consider *putting on the heat* when your opponent is slightly conservative."

Put them on (a hand). To assign a value to your opponent's hand. "Using my instincts and how he played the hand, *I put* Stanley on the nut straight."

Rag (or Blank). A board card that doesn't help you and appears not to help anyone else either. "The flop came with A-Q-4 and then a *rag*, the 8♠, hit on the turn."

Rainbow flop. The flop cards are three different suits. "I liked my straight draw when the *flop came rainbow* because I knew that nobody could have a flush draw against me."

Raise. Make an opening bet that is larger than the previous bet. "I noticed that whenever Jake had a big pocket pair in early position, he would *raise* the pot."

Reraise. Make another bet after an opponent has already raised the pot. "Claudia raised to $20 in front of me and I *reraised* it to $40."

Rake. The amount of money the house charges players to run the game. "In the $4-$8 limit hold'em game I was playing, the house *rake* was $3 per pot."

Read the board. Understand the value of your hand in relation to the cards on the board. "If you *read the board* correctly, you often can tell where you're at in the hand by the action."

Read an opponent. To put your opponent on the correct hand. "I just knew that Shane had pocket aces when she raised Tom. Sure enough, I had *read her* perfectly."

Rebuy event. If you go broke early in the tournament, you can buy more chips (usually during the first three rounds only). "I made three $100 rebuys in the $100 limit hold'em *rebuy event.*"

River. The fifth and final community card in flop games such as hold'em. "I caught an ace on the *river* and beat my opponent's kings and tens with aces and kings."

Round. When the button has gone completely around the table. "From the small blind through the button, I sat through the entire *round* without getting a playable hand." Also, the predetermined length of time each betting increment is in force during a tournament. "After the third *round* of play in a rebuy event, you cannot make any further rebuys or add-ons."

Runner-runner. To catch cards on the turn and river that make your hand a winner. "As it turns out, you had a suited K-J, caught *runner-runner* to make a flush, and broke me!"

Showdown. When the cards are turned over on the river to determine the winner. "If everyone checks to you at the river and you couldn't win in a *showdown*, why bet if you know that you will get called?"

Shut down. Discontinue aggressive action. "When the board paired the second highest card, I decided to *shut down*."

Slow-play. To intentionally not bet a strong hand for maximum value because you are hoping to trap your opponents. "I knew the rock in the third seat was *slow-playing* aces so I didn't bet my set when he checked on the flop."

Smooth call. Call a bet without raising. "If someone bets into you, you might *smooth call* with this type of hand because you have an extra out."

Solid player. An accomplished player who employs optimal strategy at all times. "I decided not to call Boston's raise because I knew he was a *solid player* who wouldn't get out of line."

Stand a raise. Call a raise. "I recently *stood a raise* in a cash game with 9-8 on the button. The board came 7-6-2, no suits. A guy led off with a decent bet and I called him with my overcards and a straight draw."

Surrender. Give up on your hand. Fold. "When the fourth flush card hit at the river, I had to *surrender*."

Survival tactics. Playing conservatively rather than betting for maximum value in an attempt to last longer in a tournament. "My chip count was so low I decided to use *survival tactics* to give myself a chance to win."

Take off a card. Call a bet on the flop. "I decided to *take off a card* and see what the turn would bring."

Tell. A playing habit that a player consistently uses at the table which enables his opponent to tell what he is holding or predict what he is likely to do during the play of a hand. "I noticed right away that when John had a weak hand, he fidgeted with his chips. I used that *tell* against him and raised when he bet from early position."

Tilt (on). Playing too loose and aggressively, especially after suffering a few bad beats. "After getting beaten on the last two hands when somebody drew out on him, Brad went *on tilt* and raised the pot three times in a row with trash hands."

Turn (card). The fourth community card. "I made a straight on the *turn* and raised the pot. Unfortunately, Cathy snagged a flush card on the river to beat me."

Under the gun. The first player sitting to the left of the big blind. "I couldn't believe it when Mark showed the pair of fours that he had raised with *under the gun*."

Wake up with a hand. To be dealt a hand with winning potential. "Just because a player is a maniac doesn't mean that he can't *wake up with a hand*. Over the long haul, everybody gets the same number of good hands and bad hands."

Weak Ace.
To have an ace in your hand but you don't have a high kicker to go with it. "I won't call with a *weak ace* unless I'm the big blind and the pot hasn't been raised."

Where you're at (in a hand). To understand the value of your hand in relation to the other players' hands. "Your opponent may not know for sure *where you're at in the hand* when you play it in a deceptive way."

THE CHAMPIONSHIP SERIES

POWERFUL BOOKS YOU MUST HAVE

CHAMPIONSHIP STUD (Seven-Card Stud, Stud 8/or Better and Razz) by Dr. Max Stern, Linda Johnson, & Tom McEvoy. The authors, who have earned millions of dollars in major tournaments and cash games, eight World Series of Poker bracelets and hundreds of other titles in competition against the best players in the world show you the winning strategies for medium-limit side games as well as poker tournaments and a general tournament strategy that is applicable to any form of poker. Includes give-and-take conversations between the authors to give you more than one point of view on how to play poker. 200 pages, hand pictorials, photos. $29.95.

CHAMPIONSHIP OMAHA (Omaha High-Low, Pot-limit Omaha, Limit High Omaha) by T. J. Cloutier & Tom McEvoy. Clearly-written strategies and powerful advice from Cloutier and McEvoy who have won four World Series of Poker titles in Omaha tournaments. Powerful advice shows you how to win at low-limit and high-stakes games, how to play against loose and tight opponents, and the differing strategies for rebuy and freezeout tournaments. Learn the best starting hands, when slowplaying a big hand is dangerous, what danglers are and why winners don't play them, why pot-limit Omaha is the only poker game where you sometimes fold the nuts on the flop and are correct in doing so and overall, how you can win a lot of money at Omaha! 230 pages, photos, illustrations, $39.95. Now only $29.95!

CHAMPIONSHIP TOURNAMENT POKER by Tom McEvoy. New Cardoza Edition! Rated by pros as best book on tournaments ever written and enthusiastically endorsed by more than 5 world champions, this is the definitive guide to winning tournaments and a must for every player's library. McEvoy lets you in on the secrets he has used to win millions of dollars in tournaments and the insights he has learned competing against the best players in the world. Packed solid with winning strategies for all 11 games in the World Series of Poker, with extensive discussions of 7-card stud, limit hold'em, pot and no-limit hold'em, Omaha high-low, re-buy, half-half tournaments, satellites, strategies for each stage of tournaments. Tons of essential concepts and specific strategies jam-pack the book. Phil Hellmuth, 1989 WSOP champion says, [this] is the world's most definitive guide to winning poker tournaments. 416 pages, paperback, $29.95.

THE CHAMPIONSHIP SERIES
POWERFUL BOOKS YOU <u>MUST</u> HAVE

CHAMPIONSHIP TABLE (at the World Series of Poker) by Dana Smith, Ralph Wheeler, & Tom McEvoy. New Cardoza Edition! From 1970 when the champion was presented a silver cup, to the present when the champion was awarded more than $2 million, Championship Table celebrates three decades of poker greats who have competed to win poker's most coveted title. This book gives you the names and photographs of all the players who made the final table, pictures the last hand the champion played against the runner-up, how they played their cards, and how much they won. This book also features fascinating interviews and conversations with the champions and runners-up and interesting highlights from each Series. This is a fascinating and invaluable resource book for WSOP and gaming buffs. In some cases the champion himself wrote "how it happened," as did two-time champion Doyle Brunson when Stu Ungar caught a wheel in 1980 on the turn to deprive "Texas Dolly" of his third title. Includes tons of vintage photographs. 208 pages, paperback, $19.95.

CHAMPIONSHIP NO-LIMIT & POT-LIMIT HOLD'EM by T. J. Cloutier & Tom McEvoy. New Cardoza Edition! The definitive guide to winning at two of the world's most exciting poker games! Written by eight time World Champion players T. J. Cloutier (1998 and 2002 Player of the Year) and Tom McEvoy (the foremost author on tournament strategy) who have won millions of dollars each playing no-limit and pot-limit hold'em in cash games and major tournaments around the world. You'll get all the answers here - no holds barred - to your most important questions: How do you get inside your opponents' heads and learn how to beat them at their own game? How can you tell how much to bet, raise, and reraise in no-limit hold'em? When can you bluff? How do you set up your opponents in pot-limit hold'em so that you can win a monster pot? What are the best strategies for winning no-limit and pot-limit tournaments, satellites, and supersatellites? You get rock-solid and inspired advice from two of the most recognizable figures in poker — advice that you can bank on. If you want to become a winning player, a champion, you must have this book. 288 pages, paperback, illustrations, photos. $29.95.

THE CHAMPIONSHIP SERIES
POWERFUL BOOKS YOU <u>MUST</u> HAVE

CHAMPIONSHIP SATELLITE STRATEGY by Brad Dougherty & Tom McEvoy. In 2002 and 2003 satellite players won their way into the $10,000 WSOP buy-in and emerged as champions, winning more than $2 million each. You can too! You'll learn specific, proven strategies for winning almost any satellite. Learn the 10 ways to win a seat at the WSOP and other big tournaments, how to win limit hold'em and no-limit hold'em satellites, one-table satellites for big tournaments, and online satellites, plus how to play the final table of super satellites. McEvoy and Daugherty sincerely believe that if you practice these strategies, you can win your way into any tournament for a fraction of the buy-in. You'll learn how much to bet, how hard to pressure opponents, how to tell when an opponent is bluffing, how to play deceptively, and how to use your chips as weapons of destruction. Includes a special chapter on no-limit hold'em satellites! 256 pages. Illustrated hands, photos, glossary. $24.95.

CHAMPIONSHIP PRACTICE HANDS by T. J. Cloutier & Tom McEvoy. Two tournament legends show you how to become a winning tournament player. Get inside their heads as they think they way through the correct strategy at 57 limit and no-limit practice hands. Cloutier & McEvoy show you how to use your skill and intuition to play strategic hands for maximum profit in real tournament scenarios and how 45 key hands were played by champions in turnaround situations at the WSOP. By sharing their analysis on how the winners and losers played key hands, you'll gain tremendous insights into how tournament poker is played at the highest levels. Learn how champions think and how they play major hands in strategic tournament situations, Cloutier and McEvoy believe that you will be able to win your share of the profits in today's tournaments -- and join them at the championship table far sooner than you ever imagined. 288 pages, illustrated with card pictures, $29.95.

CARDOZA PUBLISHING
ORDER FORM

Name _____

Address _____

City _____ State _____ Zip _____

Daytime Telephone Number _____

Quantity	Your Order	Price	

	Subtotal		
	Postage/Handling: First Item - 5.00	5	00
	Additional Postage		
	(NY residents add 8.25%)		
	Total Amount Due		

MAKE CHECKS PAYABLE TO:
Cardoza Publishing
P.O. Box 1500, Cooper Station
New York, NY 10276

CHARGE BY PHONE: (9:00-5:30 EST)
Toll-Free: 1-800-577-WINS
E-Mail Orders: CardozaPub@aol.com

SHIPPING CHARGES
U.S. ORDERS • Where shipping is specified, enclose that amount and $1 extra for each additional item; when shipping is not specified, include $5 for the first item ordered, $1 each additional.
HAWAII/ALASKA/PUERTO RICO • Triple U.S. costs for shipping.
CANADA/MEXICO • Double U.S. costs for books, strategies, software; triple other products.
OTHER COUNTRIES • Quadruple (4x) U.S. costs for all products.
Orders outside U.S., send money order payable in U.S. dollars on U.S. bank only.

0-day money back guarantee on all orders (software and personalized items excluded). Returned items must be in saleable condition. There is a 15% restocking fee on returns. Prices subject to change.

CREDIT CARD ORDERS

MC/VISA/AMEX/DIS # _____ Expiration Date _____

Signature _____

ORDER BY PHONE NOW • 1-800-577-WINS
MC/VISA/AMEX/DISCOVER
Order Desk Open 9:00-5:30 EST Eastern Standard Time

POWERFUL POKER SIMULATIONS
A MUST FOR SERIOUS PLAYERS WITH A COMPUTER!
IBM compatible CD ROM Win 95, 98, 2000, NT, ME, XP
Full Color Graphics

Play interactive poker against these **incredible** full color poker simula programs—they're the absolute **best** method to improve your game. Compu players act like real players. All games let you set the limits and rake, have fu programmable players, adjustable lineup, stat tracking, and Hand Analy for starting hands. Mike Caro, the world's foremost poker theoretician sa "Amazing... a steal for under $500... get it, it's great." Includes free teleph support. **New Feature!** - "Smart Advisor" gives expert advice for every p in every game!

1. TURBO TEXAS HOLD'EM FOR WINDOWS - $89.95 - Choose w players, how many, 2-10, you want to play, create loose/tight game, cor check-raising, bluffing, position, sensitivity to pot odds, more! Also, ins replay, pop-up odds, Professional Advisor, keeps track of play statistics. F bonus: Hold'em Hand Analyzer analyzes all 169 pocket hands in detail, t win rates under any conditions you set. Caro says this "hold'em softwar the most powerful ever created." Great product!

2. TURBO SEVEN-CARD STUD FOR WINDOWS - $89.95 - Cre any conditions of play; choose number of players (2-8), bet amounts, fi or spread limit, bring-in method, tight/loose conditions, position, reactio board, number of dead cards, stack deck to create special conditions, ins replay. Terrific stat reporting includes analysis of starting cards, 3-D bar cha graphs. Play interactively, run high speed simulation to test strategies. H Analyzer analyzes starting hands in detail. Wow!